STEP INTO WRITING

Your guide to writing, punctuation and grammar

WILLIAM CASEY

Gill & Macmillan
Hume Avenue
Park West
Dublin 12
with associated companies throughout the world
www.gillmacmillan.ie

ISBN: 978 07171 56641

© William Casey 2013

Design: Design Image
Internal illustrations: Derry Dillon
Cover design: Slick Fish Design

Printed by Brunswick Press Limited, Dublin

The paper used in this book comes from the wood pulp of managed forests. For every tree felled, at least one tree is planted, thereby renewing natural resources.

All rights reserved. No part of this publication may be copied, reproduced or transmitted in any form or by any means, without written permission of the publishers or else under the terms of any licence permitting limited copying issued by the Irish Copyright Licensing Agency.

Any links to external websites should not be construed as an endorsement by Gill & Macmillan of the content or view of the linked material.

For permission to reproduce photographs and text extracts, the author and publisher gratefully acknowledge the following:
© Alamy: 5C, 33R, 49, 56C, 56B, 121, 140, 146R, 155T, 155B; © Getty Images: 7, 8C, 26C, 52T, 52B, 53, 54, 55L, 58, 60, 61, 62, 64, 65, 65, 67, 68, 70, 76, 80, 84, 87, 90, 95, 98, 103, 106, 117T, 120, 125T, 128, 129, 135T, 137, 142, 146L, 154, 156, 160, 169R, 171R, 178, 181, 185, 187T, 188B, 188T, 192, 196, 199, 204, 207B; © Photocall Ireland: 5TL; © Shutterstock: 2, 5TL, 5TR, 5CB, 5BT, 5B, 6, 8B, 9, 13, 13, 15, 16, 19, 21, 23, 25, 25, 26B, 26T, 27, 29, 33L, 34, 35, 36, 37, 38, 41, 41, 43, 47, 47, 48, 50, 55R, 56T, 79, 81, 85, 88, 96, 102, 105, 112, 118, 122, 125B, 130, 135B, 141, 145, 149, 157, 168, 169L, 171L, 174, 180, 184, 186, 187B, 188C, 191, 195, 197, 201, 207T, 208; Courtesy of Irish Guide Dogs for the Blind: 135.

'A Victorian Schoolmistress's 10 Golden Rules of Punctuation' reprinted by permission of HarperCollins Publishers Ltd © 1999, Graham King. 'First Day Back' by June Crebbin, published in *The Dinosaur's Dinner*, 1992. 'The Sound Collector' from *Pillow Talk* by Roger McGough © 1990 Viking-Penguin reprinted by permission of Peters Fraser & Dunlop (www.petersfraserdunlop.com) on behalf of Roger McGough. 'Camping' by Natasha Niemi © My Word Wizard. 'Recipe for a story' © Michaela Morgan, first published in *How to Teach Poetry at KS2*. Blurb from *Diary of a Wimpy Kid: Roderick Rules* (Puffin, 2009) © Jeff Kinney, 2008. *The Twits* © Roald Dahl (Jonathan Cape Ltd & Penguin Books Ltd). 'All My Great Excuses.' © 2007 by Kenn Nesbitt. Reprinted from *Revenge of the Lunch Ladies* with the permission of Meadowbrook Press.

The author and publisher have made every effort to trace all copyright holders, but if any has been inadvertently overlooked we would be pleased to make the necessary arrangement at the first opportunity.

CONTENTS

Note for teachers vi
Acknowledgments viii

Section A Grammar

The parts of speech 2
- Nouns 5
- Pronouns 10
- Verbs 12
- Adjectives 16
- Adverbs 20
- Articles 22
- Prepositions 22
- Conjunctions 24
- Exclamations 25

Writing tools 26
- Antonyms 26
- Synonyms 26
- Homonyms 27
- Homophones 27
- Idioms 28
- Proverbs 29
- Compound words 30
- Prefixes 30
- Suffixes 31
- Imagery 32
- Similes 32
- Personification 33
- Metaphors 34
- Onomatopoeia 34
- Direct and indirect speech 36
- Sentences 38
- Paragraphs 42

Dialogue	45
Connectives	46
Types of texts	**47**
The parts of a text	**49**

Section B Punctuation

Punctuation	**52**
Capital letters	53
Full stops	55
Question marks	57
Brackets	59
Dashes	59
Exclamation marks	60
Hyphens	62
Apostrophes	63
Colons	66
Semicolons	67
Commas	68
Inverted commas	71
Punctuation poems	**73**
Punctuation summary	**75**

Section C Writing: Fiction and Non-fiction

Process approach to writing	**78**
Writing frames	**84**
Formal or informal language?	**86**
Letters	**87**
Formal letters	87
Informal letters	95
Addressing envelopes	101
Emails	102
Recount	**104**
Newspaper reports	116
Procedure	**121**
Information reports	**128**

Explanation	**134**
Persuasion	**140**
Leaflets and posters	146
Discussion	**148**
Response	**154**
Narrative	**159**
How to plan a character	178

Section D Poetry

Rhyme	**184**
Assonance	**186**
Rhythm	**187**
Alliteration	**188**
Writing poetry	**189**
Forms of poetry	**191**
Process approach to writing poetry	**192**
Using poetry to write poetry	**195**
Acrostic poem	**198**
Concrete poem	**201**
Cinquain	**204**
Free verse	**206**
Topic suggestions	212
Index	215

NOTE FOR TEACHERS

This book is about fiction and non-fiction writing in the classroom. It shows how teachers can use writing frames to give children a structure for their writing. This approach helps children to move towards greater independence in their writing while also familiarising them with different types of texts.

Writing frames

This book uses writing frames to teach both fiction and non-fiction writing. Writing frames are very helpful because they:

- Give the children an overview of the writing task from start to finish
- Provide an alternative to a blank sheet of paper (which can be particularly daunting for those children who find sustained writing difficult)
- Ensure some success at writing: a vital ingredient in fostering self-esteem and a motivation to write

Use of the writing frames should always follow this sequence:
1. Discussion and teacher modelling
2. Joint construction: teacher and child(ren)
3. Independent writing supported by the frame

Not all children will need to use writing frames in class. However, the writing frames are particularly useful as a support to independent writing.

Writing frames should only be used when children have a **purpose** for writing. Children should be encouraged to cross out, amend and add to the frame as suits them.

It is envisaged that teachers will spend at least **five to six weeks** in the exploration of each genre (or as prescribed in the school plan). There is no strict recommendation for which genre should be taught first. However, since recount writing is a type of writing children will be familiar with, it makes it a good genre to start with.

Regardless of the genre chosen, it is imperative that the children use the **process approach** to writing.

All the writing frames are available to download or print from www.gillmacmillan.ie/primary

Writing in the classroom

Above all, it is vital to create a classroom environment in which writing is a stimulating, enjoyable and valued activity.

One activity that is proven to be very successful in engaging children in the skill of writing is *free writing.* Free writing activities involve encouraging the children to write for approximately ten minutes on a topic chosen by themselves. This can be done about three times a week. It is important that the writing is entirely the children's own work. Approximate spelling is accepted in free writing. The teacher should not correct this work but it should be dated. Teachers can assess the writing and identify common mistakes that will influence planning for future writing lessons.

Writing is a skill and, like all skills, practice makes perfect.

Resources for teachers

The following is a list of useful resources for fiction and non-fiction writing in the classroom.

Eather, J. 'Writing Fun' website <www.writingfun.com>

Field, M. (2009) *Improve Your Punctuation and Grammar*. UK: How To Books.

Gee, R. and Watson, C. (2000) *Improve Your Punctuation (Usborne Better English)*. UK: Usborne.

Hallam, G. (1999) *CGP Years 5–6 Literacy Hour: The Tricky Bits*. UK: Coordination Group Publications Ltd (CGP).

Halligan, J. and Newman, J. (2007) *A Way With Words 5*. Dublin: CJ Fallon.

Halligan, J. and Newman, J. (2007) *A Way With Words 6*. Dublin: CJ Fallon.

Harrett, J. (2006) *Exciting Writing: Activities for 5 to 11 Year Olds*. UK: Sage.

Harrison, M. and Stuart-Clark, C. (1998) *The New Oxford Treasury of Children's Poems*. Oxford: OUP.

Hodson, P. and Jones, D. (1990) *Teaching Children to Write: The Process Approach to Writing for Literacy*. London: David Fulton.

Irving, N. (2003) *The Usborne Guide to English Punctuation*. UK: Usborne.

King, G. (2009) *Collins: Improve Your Punctuation.* UK: Collins.

Lewis, M. and Wray, D. (1995) *Developing Children's Non-Fiction Writing: Working with Writing Frames*. US: Scholastic.

Lewis, M. and Wray, D. (1997) *Writing Frames: Scaffolding Children's Non-Fiction Writing in a Range of Genres*. UK: Reading and Language Information Centre, University of Reading.

MacIver, A. (2004) *The New First Aid in English*. UK: Hodder.

Matchett, C. (2007) *Key Stage 1 English Revision Guide (Years 1 & 2)*. UK: Schofield & Sims.

Matchett, C. (2007) *Key Stage 2 English Revision Guide (Years 3–6)*. UK: Schofield & Sims.

Morgan, M. (1990) *How to Teach Poetry KS2*. UK: Letts.

Nelson Education (various authors and dates) *PM Writing Series*. UK: Nelson Education.

Shrives, C. (2011) *Grammar for Grown-Ups.* UK: Kyle Books.

Swan, M. and Walter, C. (2001) *The Good Grammar Book*. Oxford: OUP.

ACKNOWLEDGMENTS

A word of thanks to my family, cousins, friends and all the teachers who submitted samples of their pupils' work.

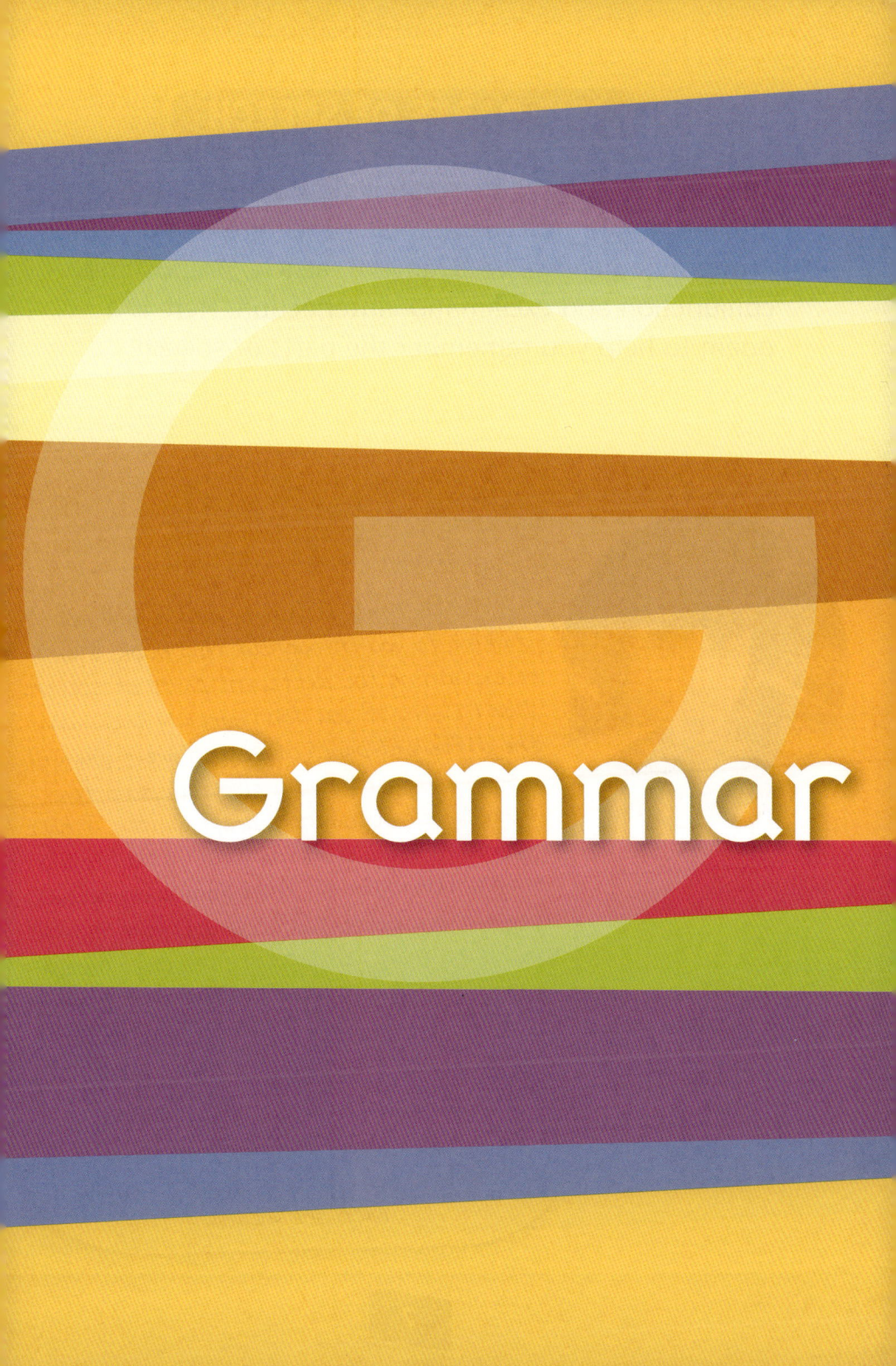

THE PARTS OF SPEECH

The parts of speech are the building blocks of the English language. The parts of speech are called noun, pronoun, adjective, verb, adverb, article, preposition, conjunction and exclamation/interjection. Here is a poem to help you remember the parts of speech.

Hi! My name is Tommy and I will be talking to you throughout this book. I will be explaining the different parts of speech. Don't worry if you don't already know what the different parts of speech are - you will soon find out! I will also tell you a few things about becoming a great writer. I have plenty of advice on that, but it's all really simple. Who knows? You might even become the next big writer! Of course, there is more to writing than just writing stories. There are many different types of writing and we'll see them all as we work through this book.

So, let's start... Did you know that all English words fall into eight main groups? These are called the parts of speech. Let's take a closer look to find out what each one means.

The Parts of Speech

Every name is called a **NOUN**,
As **field** and **fountain**, **street** and **town**.

In place of noun the **PRONOUN** stands,
As **he** and **she** can clap their hands.

The **ADJECTIVE** describes a thing,
As **magic** wand and **bridal** ring.

The **VERB** means action, something done –
To **read**, to **write**, to **jump**, to **run**.

How things are done, the **ADVERBS** tell,
As **quickly**, **slowly**, **badly**, **well**.

The **PREPOSITION** shows relation,
As **in** the street, or **at** the station.

CONJUNCTIONS join, in many ways,
Sentences, words **or** phrase **and** phrase.

The **INTERJECTION** cries out, 'Hark!
I need an exclamation mark**!**'

Through poetry, we learn how each
of these makes up **THE PARTS OF SPEECH**.

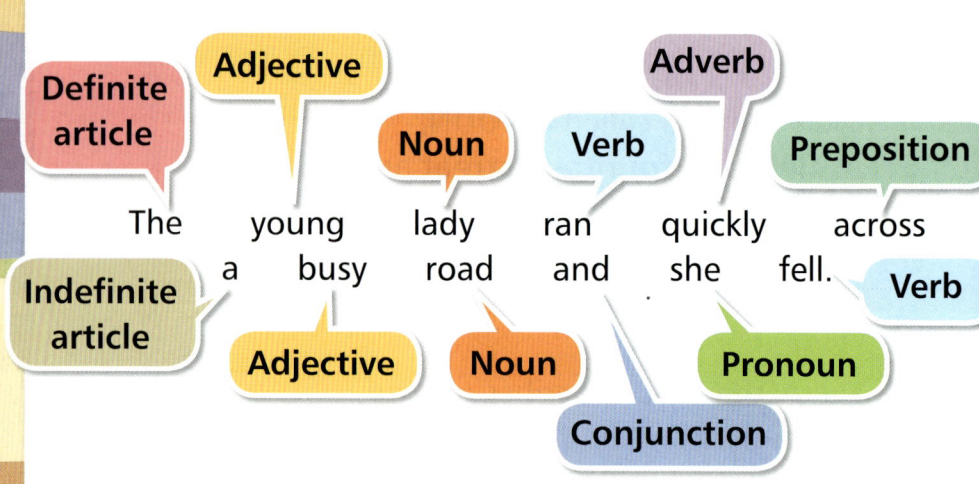

The	definite article
young	adjective
lady	noun
ran	verb
quickly	adverb
across	preposition
a	indefinite article
busy	adjective
road	noun
and	conjunction
she	pronoun
fell.	verb

Nouns

Nouns are naming words.

A noun could be the name of a person, animal, place, thing, feeling, quality or measure.

Examples of nouns

Names for people
Mary   cousin   soldier   Irishman

Names for animals
dog   lion   giraffe   cow

Names for places
house   Ireland   factory   shop

Names for things or objects
table   chair   computer   printer

Names for qualities or feelings
beauty   bravery   kindness   happiness

Names for measures
month   day   centimetre   kilogram

GRAMMAR

Types of nouns
There are different types of nouns.

Common nouns
Common nouns are words that name the everyday things around us. If we are able to touch it, smell it, see it, taste it or hear it, it is often a common noun.

> book   cake   dog   bedroom   key   bicycle

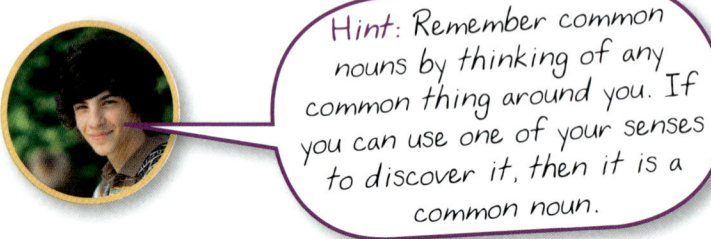

Hint: Remember common nouns by thinking of any common thing around you. If you can use one of your senses to discover it, then it is a common noun.

Proper nouns
Proper nouns are used for naming specific people, places or things. The days of the week and months of the year are also proper nouns. Proper nouns always begin with a capital letter.

> Margaret   Andrew   Cork   Mount Everest
> August   Wednesday

Abstract nouns
Abstract nouns are an idea, a feeling, a time or a quality. They cannot be seen or touched.

> love   anger   jealousy   month
> brightness   patience   freedom

Collective nouns
Collective nouns name groups of people, things or animals.

> a flock of sheep   an army of soldiers
> a troop of monkeys   a choir of singers
> a flight of stairs

Singular and plural nouns
A noun is singular if there is only one. A noun is plural if there is more than one.

For many nouns, if you want to make them plural, just add **s** at the end of the word.

Singular	Plural
dog	dogs
friend	friends

If the noun ends in a hissing sound – **ch**, **s**, **sh**, **x** or **z** – then you need to add **es** to make the plural.

Singular	Plural
witch	witches
fox	foxes

If the noun ends in **o**, just add **s** to make the plural…

Singular	Plural
piano	pianos
radio	radios

…but there are some exceptions to this rule!

Singular	Plural
potato	potatoes
tomato	tomatoes

Some nouns keep the same word for the plural…

Singular	Plural
deer	deer
sheep	sheep

…but some nouns change a lot.

Singular	Plural
foot	feet
man	men

If the noun ends in **y**, there are two things to remember for the plural.
- If the letter before the **y** is a vowel, just add **s** to make the plural.
- If the letter before the **y** is a consonant, change the **y** to **i** and add **es** to make the plural.

Singular	Plural
toy	toys
county	counties

If a noun ends in **f** or **fe**, change the **f** or **fe** to **ves** to make the plural…

Singular	Plural
half	halves
knife	knives
wolf	wolves

…but there are some exceptions to this rule!

Singular	Plural
roof	roofs
hoof	hoofs

Some nouns are always plural.

> trousers   jeans   shorts   pants
> glasses   scissors

Here is a sentence with lots of plural nouns.
- *Hannah cut her jeans with a pair of scissors to turn them into a pair of shorts.*

As you can see, there are many different types of nouns. **Remember**: you must have at least one noun or pronoun in most sentences you write.

GRAMMAR

Pronouns

Pronouns are words like *him*, *her*, *it* that take the place of nouns. We use pronouns to avoid repeating the same words over and over again.

Examples of pronouns

Singular pronouns

> I, you, he, she, it

Plural pronouns

> we, you, they

Here is an example of the same sentence written in two ways: one without pronouns and one with pronouns.

- Without pronouns: *Michelle used Michelle's mobile to call Michelle's mother.*
- With pronouns: *Michelle used **her** mobile to call **her** mother.*

In the sentence without pronouns, the writer had to keep repeating Michelle's name!

Here is another example.

- Without pronouns: *Tom bought an ice cream. Tom ate the ice cream quickly before school.*
- Without pronouns: *Tom bought an ice cream. **He** ate **it** quickly before school.*

Other pronouns include:

> me   him   her   my   mine   yours   us

Be careful with pronouns!

Pronouns are important, but if you use too many pronouns, you will confuse the reader.

Here is an example.
- *Mark left **his** dog off the lead and **he** chased the cat across the field.*

Because there are too many pronouns in this sentence, we don't know who is chasing the cat. Is it Mark or the dog?

Here is a better way to write the sentence.
- *Mark left his dog off the lead and **the dog** chased the cat across the field.*

Verbs

Verbs are **doing** and **being** words. Verbs tell us what a person or thing is doing. Almost every sentence needs at least one verb in order to make sense. Verbs set the tense of the sentence or text.

Examples of verbs
- *The children **drink** their milk and **eat** their cookies.*
- *Cillian and his friend carefully **climb** the tree.*

Other verbs include:

> walk   write   read   wander   gobble   ride
> sprint   compete   watch   jump   listen   build
> feed   pretend   whisper

Nearly all verbs are action words but there are a few that are **being** words. They tell us about something or someone – even if they don't tell us what the something or someone is doing!

Being words include:
- **Present tense**: I am, you are, he is
- **Past tense**: she was, we were
- **Future tense**: you will be, they will be

For example: The women *were* cold.
　　　　　　　The student *is* ready to start the test.

Tenses

A verb is an action word. The time of the action is called the tense. The tense of a verb can be **past**, **present** or **future**.
- **Past tense**: I jumped, I did jump, I was jumping
- **Present tense**: I jump, I am jumping
- **Future tense**: I will jump, I will be jumping

Subject–verb agreement

Hint: Before you read about subject-verb agreement, go to p. 40 and find out what 'subject' means. You already know what a verb is!

The verb must always agree with its subject. The verb form can change depending on whether the subject is singular or plural.

Here are sentences with subject–verb agreement.
- *The game shop (singular subject)* **was** *(verb) full of shoppers.*
- *The game shops (plural subject)* **were** *(verb) full of shoppers.*

*To put a verb into the past tense, we sometimes add **d** or **ed**.*
- *Present tense:* I jump
- *Past tense:* I jump**ed**

However, some verbs don't follow any rules!
- *Present tense:* I go
- *Past tense:* I went

Helper verbs
Sometimes more than one verb is used to tell us about an action.
- *Anne **is** writing her story now.*
- *Karen **has** eaten her dinner.*

Helper verbs include:

> is   was   had   were   will   has   have

Verb endings
The verb endings we add most often are **ing** and **ed**.
- jump
- jump**ing**
- jump**ed**

Rules for verb endings
If the verb ends with **e**, drop the **e** and add **ing** or **ed**.
- hope
- hop**ing**
- hop**ed**

If the verb ends with a consonant followed by **y**, change the **y** to an **i** and add **ed** to make the past tense...
- hurry
- hurr**ied**

...or keep the **y** and add **ing** to make the present tense.
- hurry
- hurry**ing**

If the verb ends in a short vowel followed by a consonant, **double the last letter** when adding **ing** or **ed**.
- hop
- ho**pp**ing
- ho**pp**ed

For verbs with a root ending in *t* or *d* (e.g. rented, shouted, landed and needed), the **ed** sounds like **id** in the past tense.

For verbs with a root ending in *p*, *k* or *f* (e.g. jumped, picked and stuffed), the **ed** sounds like *t* in the past tense.

Hint: When writing, **choose the verb** that best describes what is happening.

Here is an example of the same sentence with two different verbs.
- *After the match, the people **went** onto the streets.*
- *After the match, the people **poured** onto the streets.*

The second version is much more interesting for the reader.

Adjectives

Adjectives are words that are used to describe nouns and pronouns. Adjectives tell us more about the noun or pronoun.

Examples of adjectives
- The **hungry** girl ate a **tasty** sandwich.
- The **naughty** dog chewed the **new** sofa.

Adjectives are not always placed right beside the noun or pronoun. Sometimes adjectives appear in a different place in the sentence.
- The movie was **short** but **exciting**.

Other adjectives include:

> creepy   eerie   chilling   gloomy   salty
> smooth   fluffy   squeaky   yellow   scary   sleepy
> exhausted   powerful   nervous   late   round
> gigantic   shaky   sharp   hilarious

Comparatives and superlatives
Sometimes we need to compare adjectives.
- **Positive:** Tara is **small**.
- **Comparative:** Aoife is **smaller**.
- **Superlative:** Rachel is the **smallest**.

To make the **comparative** for most adjectives, add **er**.

To make the **superlative** for most adjectives, add **est**.

Examples of positive, comparative and superlative adjectives

Positive	Comparative	Superlative
great	great**er**	great**est**
old	old**er**	old**est**
loud	loud**er**	loud**est**
cool	cool**er**	cool**est**

The positive form of the adjective is used to describe **one** object.

The comparative form of the adjective is used to compare **two** objects.

The superlative form of the adjective is used to compare **three** or more objects.

Rules for comparatives and superlatives

If the adjective ends in a single consonant, **double it** and add **er** or **est** at the end.

Positive	Comparative	Superlative
sad	sa**dd**er	sa**dd**est
big	bi**gg**er	bi**gg**est
hot	ho**tt**er	ho**tt**est

If the adjective ends in **y**, change the **y** to **i** and add **er** or **est** at the end.

Positive	Comparative	Superlative
happy	happier	happiest
easy	easier	easiest
funny	funnier	funniest

Some words would be hard to pronounce if **er** or **est** were added, so we use **more** and **most** instead. This usually happens with adjectives of three syllables or more.

Positive	Comparative	Superlative
beautiful	**more** beautiful	**most** beautiful
famous	**more** famous	**most** famous
exciting	**more** exciting	**most** exciting

Sometimes the adjective changes completely.

Positive	Comparative	Superlative
bad	worse	worst
good	better	best
much	more	most

Numbers are sometimes called adjectives. Here is an example of a number working as an adjective.
- *Elaine has **four** brothers.*

Using adjectives in your own writing

Adjectives can really bring your writing to life! Here is an example of the same sentence written in two ways:

one without adjectives and one with adjectives.
- Without adjectives: *David looked up at the sky.*
- With adjectives: *David looked up at the **dark** and **angry** sky.*

Try to use interesting adjectives. Here is an example of the same sentence written in two ways, using different adjectives.
- *The **nice** boy made **good** sandwiches for his friends.*
- *The **kind** boy made **delicious** sandwiches for his friends.*

> Try not to use boring adjectives! Adjectives like good, nice and bad are used too often. Find synonyms to replace them, e.g. fabulous, gorgeous and horrid. If you find it tricky to think of exciting adjectives, use a thesaurus.

> Writers are like painters except they use adjectives instead of paint to create their pictures. When writing, use adjectives to add colour to your sentences in order to paint pictures in the reader's mind. This will help the reader to picture the settings, characters and events you are describing.
>
> Let's look at Roald Dahl's use of adjectives in an extract from his book *The Twits*.

A person who has **good** thoughts cannot ever be **ugly**. You can have a **wonky** nose and a **crooked** mouth and a **double** chin and **stick-out** teeth, but if you have **good** thoughts they will shine out of your face like sunbeams and you will always look **lovely**.

Adverbs

Adverbs describe verbs.

Examples of adverbs
- The monkey **quickly** grabbed the bag of peanuts.
- The class did their spellings **correctly**.

Other adverbs include:

> wildly madly greedily slowly easily
> patiently always brightly cleverly monthly
> very terribly properly mysteriously exactly
> foolishly first never simply really

Types of adverbs
Some adverbs tell us **how** something happens.
- The dog walked **slowly**.

Some adverbs tell us **when** something happens.
- I am going to the party **tomorrow**.

Some adverbs tell us **where** something happens.
- We walked **downhill** to the football pitch.

Some adverbs tell us **how often** something happens.
- I **often** listen to the radio.

Making adverbs from adjectives
Sometimes, adverbs can be made from adjectives. This is done by adding **ly** at the end of the adjective.

- He played his music **loudly**.
- The pupils **quietly** tiptoed out of the classroom.

Rules for making adverbs from adjectives
If the adjective ends in **l**, keep the **l** and add **ly**.
- careful
- carefu**ll**y

If the adjective ends in **le,** change the **e** to **y**.
- comfortable
- comfortab**ly**

If the adjective ends in a consonant followed by **e**, keep the **e** and add **ly**.
- immediate
- immediate**ly**

If the adjective ends in **y**, add **il** before the y.
- happy
- happ**il**y

Adverbs can make your writing more interesting – but be careful not to use too many of them.

Using adverbs in your own writing
The following examples show how adverbs can add information to a sentence.
- Niamh picked up the puppy.
- Niamh **carefully** picked up the puppy.
- Niamh picked up the puppy **yesterday**.
- Niamh picked up the puppy **outside**.
- Niamh picked up the puppy **once**.

Articles

The words **a**, **an** and **the** are articles. The word **the** is known as the **definite article** because it indicates a specific thing. **A** and **an** are **indefinite articles** because they do not indicate a specific thing.

Examples of definite articles
- ***The** dog ate my dinner.*
- ***The** teacher was angry with me.*

These examples refer to a specific dog and a specific teacher, so the definite article **the** is used.

Examples of indefinite articles
- ***A** dog ate my dinner.*
- *I had to give the letter to **a** teacher.*

These examples do not refer to a specific dog or a specific teacher, so the indefinite article **a** is used.

Prepositions

A preposition shows the relationship between one thing and another.

Examples of prepositions
- *Bridget stepped **on** the cat!*
- *James hid **under** the bed.*
- *Seán dived **into** the swimming pool.*

Other prepositions include:

under	between	with	about	above	across	
against	among	around	at	before	behind	
below	beneath	beside	by	down	during	
	for	from	in	into	near	of
off	on	over	through	to	towards	
		under	with	without		

If you are unsure whether or not a word is a preposition, the best thing to do is ask yourself if the word tells you about the relation between two things. If it does, it is probably a preposition.

Types of prepositions
Prepositions are about **time** and **place**.

Prepositions of time
- I watched TV **after** I had finished my homework.
- Charlie kept talking **during** the movie.

Prepositions of place
- Fifi is sitting **under** the table.
- Mark is **opposite** Joanne.
- Tricia is in **front** of Mike.
  Mike is **behind** Tricia.

Did you know?
Use **between** when talking about two things. Use **among** when talking about more than two things.
- I sat **between** Gillian and Sarah at the tennis match.
- I shared my sweets **among** my six friends.

Conjunctions

Conjunctions are used to join words or groups of words together. The most common ones are **and**, **or** and **but**.

Examples of conjunctions
- *It is warm **and** sunny today.*
- *I need help with my sums, **so** I often ask the teacher for help.*

Conjunctions can also join two sentences into one. When a conjunction is used in this way, it usually has a comma before it.
- *He is a great hurler, **but** he prefers to play golf.*

Other conjunctions include:

| although | while | despite | neither | if | either |
| or | so | until | unless | as | while |

Using conjunctions in your own writing
Try not to overuse the conjunctions **and** or **because**. It is better to arrange words into clear sentences.

Exclamations

Exclamations are words used to express a strong feeling or sudden emotion.

Examples of exclamations
- *Hey! Get off that wall!*
- *Watch out! There's a bee in your hair!*
- *Look behind you!*
- *Wow! You did well!*

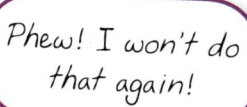

Some exclamations are sounds.

Phew! I won't do that again!

Hint: Don't use too many exclamation marks. One exclamation mark is enough to get your message across.

WRITING TOOLS

Some writing tools have unusual names, which you'll need to learn.

Antonyms

An antonym is a word that means the **opposite** of another word.

Examples of antonyms
- dark/bright
- deep/shallow
- weak/strong
- funny/serious

Synonyms

A synonym is a word that means the **same** as another word.

Examples of synonyms
- shut/close
- new/modern
- select/choose

A thesaurus is a book of synonyms.

Homonyms

Homonyms are words that have the same spelling but different meanings. They may also be pronounced differently.

Examples of homonyms
- My **left** hand is broken. I have only two chips **left**.
- You cannot **refuse** to put out the **refuse** for collection.

Homophones

Homophones are words that sound the same but have different meanings. They are also spelled differently.

Examples of homophones
- *They're* going to miss **their** bus.
- They lost **their** money over **there** near the trees.
- I can **see** the **sea**.
- The fisherman did **not** tie the **knot** carefully.

- To remember the meaning of **there**, look at the word **here** contained within **there**: *She wants to go there at the weekend.*
- To remember the meaning of **their**, think of the i as the image of a person contained in the word **their**: *That is their friend.*
- To remember the meaning of **they're**, remind yourself that the apostrophe is standing in for the letter **a** in **they are**: *They're going to meet at the park.*

It can be difficult to know when to use there, their or they're. Here's how you can remember which one to choose.

GRAMMAR

Idioms

Idioms are common phrases that most people use in conversation. You cannot work out what an idiom means by looking at the everyday meanings of the words in the idiom. You have to learn the idiom's meaning.

Examples of idioms

- *Get into hot water*
  Get into trouble

- *Face the music*
  Face the consequences

- *Keep your chin up*
  Stay happy/stay positive

- *Under the weather*
  Feeling unwell

- *Keep your hair on*
  Be patient

- *Sit on the fence*
  Not make a decision

Proverbs

A proverb is a short, clever and popular saying. It usually teaches a lesson or gives advice.

Examples of proverbs

- *Too many cooks spoil the broth.*
  It is a bad idea to have too many people working on the same task.

- *A poor workman blames his tools.*
  Some people blame others for their own failures.

- *All's well that ends well.*
  An event that has a good outcome is a good thing, even if some things go wrong along the way.

Proverbs are often short and to the point: *Practice makes perfect.*

Proverbs can provide wise advice: *Slow and steady wins the race.*

Proverbs contain simple truths: *Honesty is the best policy.*

Here are two traditional proverbs.

- Irish proverb: If you do not sow in spring you will not reap in autumn.
- Japanese proverb: One kind word can warm three winter months.

Compound words

A compound word is made when two words are joined to form a new word.

Examples of compound words
- egg + cup = eggcup
- rain + coat = raincoat
- foot + ball = football

Other compound words include:

> sunflower   teapot   grandmother   lifetime
> basketball   earthquake   underground
> keyboard   supermarket   anywhere

Prefixes

A prefix is added to the **beginning** of a word in order to make a new word. A prefix often makes the **root word** mean the **opposite**.

Examples of prefixes
- mis = not
- mis + understood = misunderstood
- mis + lead = mislead

Other prefixes include:

> **dis**respect   **dis**own   **il**legal   **un**happy   **in**edible

Suffixes

A suffix is a group of letters added to the **end** of a word. The suffix can change the meaning of the word or the way that the word is used.

Examples of suffixes
- friend + ly = friendly
- entertain + ment = entertainment

Other suffixes include:

care**ful**   enjoy**ment**   hero**ic**   kind**ness**

A suffix can change the spelling of the root word.

If the root ends in **e** and the suffix starts with a vowel, drop the **e**.
- lov**e** + **a**ble = lovable

If the root ends in **e** and the suffix starts with a consonant, keep the **e**.
- love + ly = love**ly**

If the root ends with a consonant followed by **y**, change the **y** to **i** and add the suffix.
- happy + er = happ**i**er

Imagery

Imagery is where language is used to give a clear picture (or image) of something. Imagery brings writing to life and gives the reader a clearer picture in their mind. Similes, metaphors, personification and onomatopoeia are all types of images.

Similes

A simile is a way of describing something by comparing it to something else. The word **as** or **like** is always used in a simile.

Examples of similes
- *His fingers were **as** cold **as** ice.*
- *David's shadow was enormous and frightening, **like** Frankenstein's monster.*
- *The giant was **as** tall **as** a skyscraper.*

Other similes include:

as white as snow	as busy as a bee	as slippery as an eel
as bold as brass	as old as the hills	as pale as death
as warm as wool	as dead as a doornail	as quick as lightning
as weak as water	as flat as a pancake	as heavy as lead
as dry as a bone	as cold as ice	as light as a feather

Personification

Personification means to describe an object or idea as if it were a human being.

Examples of personification

- *The little house stood strong and upright, its yellow face smiling in the warmth of the sun and its red roof a jaunty hat perched on its proud head.* (Jacqueline Harrett, *Exciting Writing*)

Let's look up the word 'jaunty' in the dictionary...

jaun·ty
Adjective:
Having or expressing a lively, cheerful and self-confident manner

- *The little stream jumped, laughing over the stones and ran cheerfully down the mountain.*

In this example, the stream is described as if it were a person jumping, laughing and running.

Metaphors

A metaphor says that one thing **actually is** something else. It makes a clear image in the reader's mind because it makes them think of the two things at once.

Examples of metaphors
- *John is a real **pig** when he eats.* This person is described as if he were a pig because of the rude way he eats.

Other metaphors include:

> The test was a walk in the park.
> He has a heart of stone.

Metaphors are very common in everyday language. Poets often use metaphors.

Onomatopoeia

Onomatopoeia is a word that mimics a sound.

Examples of onomatopoeia
- *The horse's hoofs went **clip-clop**.*
- ***Crash!** The glass **smashed** when it hit the floor.*

*Onomatopoeia is often used by poets because it allows the reader to **see** and **hear** the scene that the poet wants to describe.*

Other onomatopoeic words include:

> buzz   splish-splash   cuckoo   bang   fizz
> hiss   tick-tock   click   zip   slurp
> vroom   sizzle   crunch

Below is an example of an onomatopoeia poem. This type of poem uses words that sound just like the actual sound they are trying to describe.

Camping
by Natasha Niemi
Crack! Crack!
The fire crackles under the stars.
Sizzle! Sizzle!
The water sizzles above the fire.
Crunch! Crunch!
The campers crunching on potato chips.
Click! Clack! Click! Clack!
The tent poles clicking and clacking together.
Rustle! Rustle!
As we prepare our sleeping bags to go to sleep.
Chirp! Chirp!
The crickets say goodnight.

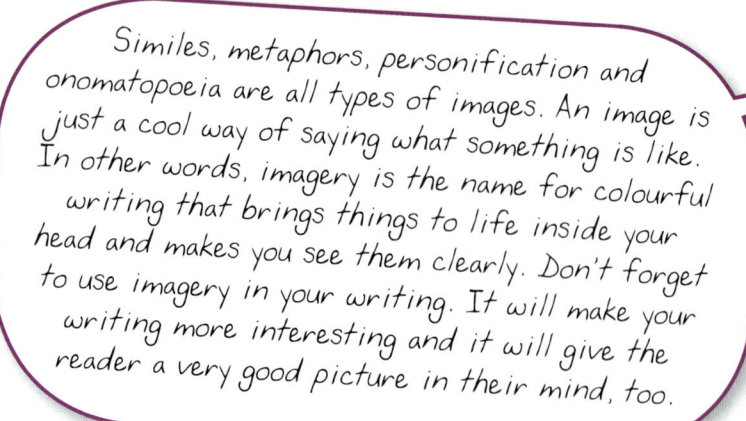

> Similes, metaphors, personification and onomatopoeia are all types of images. An image is just a cool way of saying what something is like. In other words, imagery is the name for colourful writing that brings things to life inside your head and makes you see them clearly. Don't forget to use imagery in your writing. It will make your writing more interesting and it will give the reader a very good picture in their mind, too.

Direct and indirect speech

There are two ways that you can write what a person has said.

- You can write down the exact words the person said (direct speech) and put the words in quotation marks:

  'I want to buy candyfloss at the funfair,' said Sarah.

OR

- You can use your own words to report what the person said. This is called indirect speech or reported speech. You do not use quotation marks here:

  Sarah said that she wanted to buy candyfloss at the funfair.

> Direct speech can be written in three basic ways.

- The spoken words can come at the beginning of the sentence:

  'I am so happy that I won a trophy for dancing,' said Liz.

OR

- The spoken words can come at the end of the sentence:

  Liz said, 'I am so happy that I won a trophy for dancing.'

OR

- The spoken words can come at the beginning and at the end of the sentence, with an interruption in the middle:

  'I am so happy,' said Liz, 'that I won a trophy for dancing.'

If you are writing direct speech, try not to use **says** or **said** too often. Here are some interesting words you could use instead.

mutter   ask   declare   cry   exclaim
observe   whisper   reply   comment
shout   repeat   command

Sentences

> Before we look at the different types of writing (genres), we first need to look at what every piece of writing is made of – sentences and paragraphs.

A sentence is a group of words about one complete idea. A sentence must make sense on its own. Every sentence must include a verb, start with a capital letter and end with a full stop (.), a question mark (?) or an exclamation mark (!).

Is it a sentence?

If you are unsure whether or not a group of words is a sentence, ask these questions.
- Does it make sense?
- Is it a complete thought?
- Does it begin with a capital letter?
- Does it end with a full stop, question mark or exclamation mark?

Simple sentence

This is an example of a simple sentence:
- *The ground shook.*

Compound sentence
Sometimes two complete sentences are joined together with a conjunction like **and** or **but**. These are called compound sentences.
- *Michael could not play hurling. He was injured.*
- *Michael could not play hurling because he was injured.*

Complex sentence
A complex sentence has a main clause that makes sense on its own and a subordinate clause that does not.
- *She went into the garden when the rain stopped.*

The **main clause** is Margaret went into the garden – it makes sense on its own.

The **subordinate clause** is when the rain stopped – it does not make sense on its own.

Types of sentences
There are different types of sentences. Try to use a few different types of sentences in your own writing. This will make it more interesting for the reader.

Statements
A statement gives information.
- *I'm going home early today.*

Questions
A question asks for information.
- *Who is knocking on the door?*

Commands or instructions
A command tells someone what to do. Commands and instructions speak directly to the reader.
- *Put the popcorn in the microwave for two minutes.*

Exclamations
An exclamation shows strong feeling. It is used to grab the reader's attention.
- *Be careful!*

Structure of sentences
The subject is the person or thing that the sentence is about. The verb is the doing word.

A sentence must have a subject and a verb
- The dog growled.
  dog   = subject
  growled = verb

Most sentences have a subject, a verb and an object
- Our dog eats meat every day.
  dog   = subject
  growled = verb
  meat   = object

Subject–verb agreement
We have already seen that the subject and the verb must agree in a sentence. In other words, a singular subject needs a singular form of the verb and a plural subject needs a plural form of the verb.
- *Gillian and Sarah* **are** *going to town.*
  Here, the subject is plural (Gillian and Sarah) and so too is the verb (are).

Length of sentences

The narrative text uses many complex sentences, but the information report uses mostly simple and compound sentences.

Top tips for writing a sentence

- When you are writing, think in sentences! Think each sentence in your head **before** you write it down.
- Try out different versions of your sentence. Decide which one sounds the best before you write it down.
- Remember to start the sentence with a capital letter. Put a full stop (or question mark or exclamation mark) at the end of your sentence and check if any other punctuation is needed.
- Read back over your sentence and check that it makes sense.
- Make your sentences interesting! You can do this by adding extra information, adjectives and adverbs.
- Remember the golden rules when writing a sentence:
    1. Think it
    2. Say it
    3. Write it
    4. Read it

Can I improve it? Does it sound OK?

Paragraphs

Paragraphs are groups of sentences. These sentences can be grouped together because they are about the same idea or because they all follow on from each other. The sentences in a paragraph are like pieces in a jigsaw puzzle: they are all connected and they all make up one idea or picture.

How to write a paragraph

To make a paragraph, either leave a blank line between the end of one paragraph and the start of the next, or leave a small space between the margin and the first word of your new paragraph (this is called indenting).

There are no exact rules to say where you should start a new paragraph, but a new paragraph usually comes when something changes in your narrative text (story), such as:

- When you write about **something new happening**
- When you write about a **new person**
- Every time **a new person speaks**
- When you write about **a different place**
- Whenever the story **moves in time**

Inside a paragraph

> Look carefully at your writing so that you can organise the information in each paragraph.

Start your paragraph with a **topic sentence.** This is a sentence that introduces the main point of the paragraph. Throughout the rest of the paragraph, you can explain that point further or give examples to back it up. Here is an example.

> Nana, as everyone called her, was an old woman but she was still able to get around without a walking stick. Her face had deep wrinkles and her hair was dyed a dark colour. Despite her age, she still loved to dance, cycle and work in her garden.

In this example, the topic sentence introduces the character of Nana, which is the main point of the paragraph. The rest of the sentences in the paragraph tell us more about the character. All the sentences in the paragraph are about the same idea – Nana.

PARAGRAPH WRITING FRAME

A good paragraph is made up of different types of sentences (some long and some short) that all express one connected idea.

Topic sentence
This sentence introduces the main point of the paragraph.

Start a **new paragraph** when something changes in the narrative text (story) such as:
- Something new happens
- A new character is introduced
- A new character speaks
- The story moves to a different place
- The story moves to a different time

Indent or leave a blank line so that the reader knows you are starting a new paragraph.

The ideas in each paragraph should be **linked** in some way to the ones in the paragraph **before** and the ones in the paragraph **after**.

To make a paragraph, either leave a blank line between the end of one paragraph and the start of the next, or leave a small space between the margin and the first word of your new paragraph (this is called indenting).

Use a **connective** at the start of paragraphs. This shows the link between the ideas in the last paragraph and the new one.

In the rest of the paragraph, you can explain your point further or give examples to back it up.

Dialogue

Dialogue is another important part of story writing. Dialogue or conversation between characters can be used to show what is happening in the story or to give information about the characters. We learn a lot about characters from **what** they say and **how** they say it.

Dialogue can be written as direct speech or indirect speech. Direct speech is useful if you want to show the reader something about the characters. Indirect speech is useful if you want to quickly summarise what was said.

Rules for writing dialogue

- Remember to use the correct punctuation.
- When a person starts to speak, always begin a new paragraph.
- Each person's speech is one paragraph, even if they only say a single word.
- When the dialogue is finished and you want to return to the narrative, start a new paragraph.
- Try not to overuse **says** or **said**. There are other words to choose from: chuckled, shrieked, moaned, etc.
- Use an adverb in your dialogue to show how a character says something:
  *he said **coldly**; he said **nervously**; he said **miserably**.*
- A script for a play or film is made up mostly of **dialogue**, with some stage directions. When writing dialogue for a play or film, inverted commas are not used (see p. 66).

Connectives

If you think of your story as a chain, then each link in the chain is a paragraph. It is important that the links are all connected. Therefore, when starting a new paragraph, it is important to tell the reader that a change in time or place has occurred. We use **connectives** to show this.

Time connectives

You will need to use time connectives when writing **stories**, **recounts** and some **explanations**.

Time connectives include:

> just then   in the end   afterwards   before
> until then   meanwhile   earlier   at the same time
> later   prior to this

Cause and effect connectives

Cause and effect connectives show how one event results in something else happening.

Cause and effect connectives include:

> as a result   consequently   therefore
> because   as   since

Contrasting or balancing connectives

You will need to use contrasting or balancing connectives when writing **discussion** or **persuasive** texts.

Contrasting or balancing connectives include:

> however   in contrast   whereas   on the other hand
> although   despite this

Hint: Use connectives in your writing to show how your ideas link together. This will make your writing flow. Remember that good writing is like a chain: it is all connected together.

TYPES OF TEXTS

Here are some interesting words you need to know in order to be an informed writer.

Biography
A biography is the story of a person's life, which is written by someone else.

Autobiography
An autobiography is when you write the story of your own life.

Novel
A novel is a long story, usually divided into chapters. A novel fills a whole book and it is one story. Novels don't have pictures.

You can also have a whole book filled with several different stories. This is called a **collection of short stories**.

Synopsis

A synopsis is another word for a summary. A synopsis of a story tells you the main events of the story in a shortened form.

> Before I look at a film on TV, I read the synopsis in the TV guide. That way, I can find out what will happen in the film and I can decide whether or not I want to watch it.

Blurb

A blurb tells you in shortened form what a book is about. Of course, it won't tell you the ending – that would spoil things! The blurb is written by the people who have published the book. Blurbs are written in a positive way in order to make you want to read the book.

Here is an example of a blurb for *Diary of a Wimpy Kid*.

Diary of a Wimpy Kid: Rodrick Rules is the second title in the bestselling *Diary of a Wimpy Kid* series.

It's a brand-new year and a brand-new journal and Greg is keen to put the humiliating (and secret!) events of last summer firmly behind him. But someone knows everything – someone whose job it is to most definitely not keep anything embarrassing of Greg's private – his big brother, Rodrick. How can Greg make it through this new school year with his cool(ish) reputation intact?

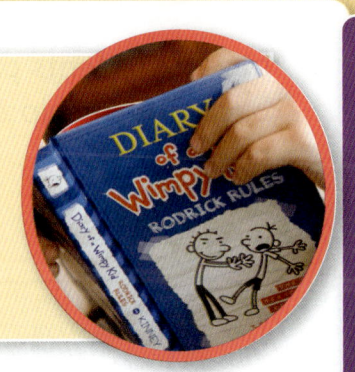

Review

Reviews are written about stories, books, plays, films and music. A review gives you information on the item being reviewed. It also tells you the reviewer's personal opinion and what they thought of the item being reviewed.

THE PARTS OF A TEXT

Every text is made up of different parts or elements. Here are some things you might find in a text.

Chapters

A novel is broken into pieces and each piece is called a chapter. Each chapter in a novel tells you part of the story.

Tables of contents

The table of contents at the start of the book tells you what each chapter is about. Non-fiction books often have a contents page at the front **and** an index at the back. These help the reader to find the pages they need.

Extracts

An extract is a piece of text taken out of a larger text.

Quotations

Quotations are a few words or lines taken from a text.

Here is a quotation from the poem 'A Smile' by Fez Mhorough.

> Smiling is infectious,
> You catch it like the flu.
> When someone smiled at me today
> I started smiling too.

Using quotations in your own writing

When you are writing a quote, you must put the speech inside quotation marks to show the reader that it is a quote – and not your own words. When you are quoting another person, it is really important that you copy the words exactly.

Punctuation

> Hi! My name is Emma and I will be telling you about punctuation. Punctuation marks are the marks used to separate words so that a writer's meaning is clear. If you want to be a writer, you need to use punctuation marks (like full stops and commas) so that the reader can easily understand what you are trying to say.

PUNCTUATION

Punctuation marks are the marks that break up words into sentences and make them easier to read. Punctuation helps to make the meaning clear. It tells the reader when to slow down (,), when to stop (.), when someone is speaking (' '), when a question is being asked (?) and when someone exclaims something (!).

Punctuation makes your writing **easier to read** but you must be careful where you put the punctuation marks.

Here is an example of the same sentence punctuated in two different ways.
- *Let's eat, Sarah!*
- *Let's eat Sarah!*

There is only one difference in the way these two sentences are punctuated – a comma. However, this comma makes a massive difference in the meaning of the sentences. In the first sentence, the speaker is asking Sarah to share a meal. In the second sentence, the speaker is talking to another person – and it sounds like they are planning to eat the girl called Sarah!

> Punctuation marks on a page are similar to signs on a road: they guide and direct you.

Capital letters

Capital letters are used at the start of a sentence. They are also used for **proper nouns**. Capital letters are also called upper case letters.

When to use capital letters

Use a capital letter at the **start of a sentence**.
- *The fox belongs to the dog family.*

Use a capital letter for **people's names**.
- *Emma and Abbie like to feed the ducks at the pond.*

Use a capital letter for **people's titles**.
- *Mr and Mrs Larkin have an appointment with Dr Roche.*

Use a capital letter for **places**.
- *Dublin is my favourite city.*

Use a capital letter for **days of the week**.
- *We get no homework on Fridays.*

Use a capital letter for **months of the year**.
- *Our summer holiday starts in June.*

Use a capital letter for **special days**.
- *At last – Christmas Day had arrived.*

Use a capital letter for **organisations**.
- *I support Manchester United.*

Use a capital letter for **titles of books, plays, etc**.
- *Artemis Fowl is written by Eoin Colfer.*

Use a capital letter for the word 'I'.
- *I enjoy playing tennis.*

Use a capital letter at the start of direct speech:
- *Mary said, 'Pancakes with lemon and sugar are delicious.'*

You can put a whole word in capital letters if you really want to make it stand out. When this is used in direct speech, it is like the speaker is shouting.
- *'HELP!'*

Capital letters are used at the beginning of so many names for so many different things: planets, departments, clubs, companies, institutions, bridges, buildings, monuments, parks, ships, hotels and streets.

Hint: You will use capital letters very often. It is most important that you remember to use capital letters: at the start of sentences, for the names of people and places, when you are writing the word 'I' and for the titles of books, plays and films.

Full stops

You need a full stop in order to end a sentence. (Sometimes we use a question mark or an exclamation mark to end a sentence. You will learn about this later.)

Examples of full stops
- *The witch flew across the sky.*
- *The teacher forgot to ring the bell at the end of break time.*

Hint: A full stop at the end of a sentence says, 'STOP!'

Types of full stops
Full stops that shorten words
Some words do not have to be written in full. You can shorten the words by writing just some of the letters or just the first (initial) letters.

Shortened words are sometimes called **abbreviations**. An abbreviation uses just some of the letters of the word. A full stop is used at the end of the abbreviation.
- Reverend = Rev.
- February = Feb.

There is another kind of abbreviation that is called a **contraction**. Contractions do not need a full stop at the end. This is because the shortened version ends with the same letter as the original word.

PUNCTUATION

- Mister = Mr
- Saint = St

Full stops and time
You can use a full stop if you are using numbers to show the time.
- *School starts at 9.00am.*

When not to use full stops
You do not need to use a full stop at the end of every line in a **notice**, **list** or **label**.

If you write a sentence that **ends with an abbreviation**, you do not need to put in two full stops – the full stop at the end of the abbreviation will be enough to end the sentence.
- *John works for Murphy & Co.*

Abbreviations of metric measurement don't need full stops: millimetres (**mm**), centimetres (**cm**) and kilometres (**km**).
- *Brian ran 10**km** on Saturday morning.*

Sometimes, well-known places or organisations are abbreviated to become **acronyms** or **initialisms**.

An **acronym** is made when the first letters of words are put together in a shortened form. They are put in capital letters without full stops. They can be pronounced like a word.
- North Atlantic Treaty Organization = NATO (pronounced 'nay-toe')

An **initialism** is made when the first letters of words are put together in a shortened form. They are put in capital letters without full stops. They cannot be pronounced like a word, so you say the letters instead.
- United States = US

Question marks

A question mark is used at the end of a sentence that asks a question. The question mark is used instead of a full stop.

Examples of questions
A question can be just one word in a sentence by itself.
- *Why?*
- *Who?*
- *How?*
- *When?*
- *What?*

Questions can also be longer, with more detail.
- *What is your favourite dessert?*
- *Where do you live?*

- *Why is water wet?*
- *Which game do you prefer?*
- *When are we going to the cinema?*
- *Do you watch* The Simpsons?

Types of questions
Direct questions
When the word or words in the sentence make a question, it is called a **direct question**. A direct question expects an answer.
- *When are we doing the history test?*
- *Did you get my text message?*

Indirect questions
An indirect question is a sentence that does not ask a question directly, but it tells you what question was asked. An indirect question does **not** have a question mark.
- *She asked when we were doing the history test.*
- *He asked me if I got his text message.*

Even if a sentence begins with one of the question words, this does not always mean it is a question.
- **When** *it is sunny I like to wear shorts.*

Even though this sentence begins with the word 'when' it is not actually a question!

Hint: Pay attention to question marks! A question mark tells you that the sentence is asking something. You must read questions with a 'question' tone of voice.

Brackets

You can use brackets to bring something extra into a sentence. This could be an explanation, an afterthought or an interruption. Brackets must always be used in pairs. They simply go around the extra words – this keeps them separate from the main sentence.

Examples of brackets
- *The streets were deserted (it was Christmas Day) and not a single shop was open.*
- *I gave the stray dog a biscuit (it was all I had left).*
- *I spoke to Dave (he is a vet) about my sick cat.*

Sometimes a whole sentence can be put into brackets. In this case, put the full stop **inside** the second bracket.
- *Use scissors to cut out the shapes. (You may need to ask an adult to help you.)*

Dashes

Dashes can be used instead of brackets.

Examples of dashes
A single dash can be used to add extra information to the end of a sentence.
- *Gran made us dinner – it was delicious.*
- *I tried to eat the broccoli – it tasted horrible.*

A dash can be used for dramatic effect. It gives the reader a feeling of suspense before a surprise.
- *I took the key and quickly tried it in the lock – it worked!*

A dash can create a pause before a surprise.

A dash can be used in dates or other expressions. You can read the dash as the word '**to**' in these expressions.
- 1965–1980

Exclamation marks

When you write a sentence that shows surprise or a sentence that might be said loudly, put an exclamation mark at the end. An exclamation mark makes a strong sentence. Exclamation marks take the place of full stops in sentences.

Types of exclamation marks
Exclamation marks show **surprise**, **humour** or **joy**.
- *Wow!*
- *Silly me!*
- *The teacher is in a bad mood!*

Exclamation marks show **fear, anger, pain** or **danger**.
- *Ouch!*
- *Watch out!*
- *I'm so scared!*

Exclamation marks are used when someone is **giving an order** or **shouting**.
- *Stop talking!*
- *Stand up!*
- *Get into the car!*

Rules for using exclamation marks
- Use the exclamation mark if you want your sentence to be strong.
- Do not use more than one exclamation mark at a time.
- Do not use exclamation marks in formal letters.

> An exclamation mark tells you that the sentence is loud or surprising. A sentence with an exclamation mark must be read with feeling!

Hyphens

The hyphen is half the length of a dash. It is a linking mark that joins two or more words together to make **one word** or **expression**. When two or more words are joined together they are called a **compound** word. Sometimes compound words have a hyphen between the two words.

Examples of hyphens

- ironing + board = ironing-board
- part + time = part-time
- twenty + three = twenty-three
- three + quarters = three-quarters

You can use a hyphen to make a group of words into a single expression.

- do-it-yourself

Sometimes you will see the same word appearing with hyphens and without – and neither version is incorrect. It's best to check a dictionary if you are unsure whether or not to add a hyphen. If it is correct both ways (with a hyphen and without), then choose one version for your writing and stick with it!

You can use a hyphen to write **numbers** and **fractions** that are more than one word. For example: *sixty-five and three-quarters; we ate three-quarters of the pie*.

Apostrophes

An apostrophe looks like a comma but it is placed at the top of letters rather than at the bottom.
- cats,   (comma)
- cat's   (apostrophe)

Examples of apostrophes

Apostrophes can be used in contractions. They can also be used to show possession (when something or someone owns something else).

Contractions

The apostrophe can be used to show that some letters have been left out of a word. This is called a **contraction**. The apostrophe goes in where the letters come out!
- don't   =   do not
- we're   =   we are
- he'll   =   he will

Other examples include:
- *Her **dog is** at the door*   =   *Her **dog's** at the door*
- *I **cannot** see it*   =   *I **can't** see it*
- *You **are** my best friend*   =   *You're my best friend*
- *I **am** writing my story*   =   *I'm writing my story*
- *We **have** a lot of homework tonight*   =   *We've a lot of homework tonight*

PUNCTUATION

Hint: Contractions (he's, she's, isn't, I'd, etc.) are common in spoken English. Be careful not to use them in formal writing. You can use them in informal writing if you are writing a message, text or a letter to a friend. You can also use them to record what someone has said (dialogue).

Possession

An apostrophe goes after the owner's name to show that something belongs to him or her.

If the owner is singular (one person), put the apostrophe at the end of the word and add an **s**.
- *This is Michael's cat.*
- *This is Aoife's coat.*

If the owner is plural (more than one), just add an apostrophe after the **s** that is already there.
- *The thief stole the ladies' handbags.*
- *The boys' football boots were new.*

If the plural does not end in **s,** just add an apostrophe and **s**.
- *The waiter went to get the men's coats.*
- *The children's parents came to see the football match.*

There is an exception to the rule! If the noun is **singular** (one person) and it ends in **s**, you can add an apostrophe after the **s** OR you can add apostrophe and s.

Let's try this with **Charles**, which is a singular name that ends in **s**.

- *It is Charles' birthday.*
- *It is Charles's birthday.*

Both versions are correct, so you just need to choose one and stick with it!

> **How to spot possessives**
> If you want to know whether or not a noun with an s needs an apostrophe, try using *of* in the sentence. For example, if you see 'John's cat' in a sentence, ask yourself if you can include the word 'of'.
> In this case, you can! 'John's cat' is 'the cat of John'. This means that the word is possessive and it needs an **apostrophe** and **s**.

The difference between *it's* and *its*

It's (with an apostrophe) means 'it is' or 'it has'.
- **It's** time we all went home. (it's = it is)
- **It's** been a very long day. (it's = it has)

In the examples above, the apostrophe is showing that letters have been left out.

Its (without an apostrophe) has a different meaning. The word 'its' shows that 'it' owns something.
- *The dog wants **its** dinner.*

This tells us that the dog **owns** its dinner.
- *The tree lost **its** leaves.*

This tells us that the tree **owns** its leaves.

> **Hint:**
> - If you are writing a short form of *it has* or *it is*, then use *it's*.
> - If you are saying 'it' owns something, then use *its*.

PUNCTUATION

Colons

Colons and semicolons (like commas and full stops) mark the places where you would break or pause when speaking.

A **colon** can be used to introduce something. The wording before the colon should introduce whatever it is that follows.

You can use a colon to: (a) introduce **lists** (b) introduce **explanations** and (c) introduce **dialogue in a script**.

Introducing lists
Colons are used to let the reader know that a list is about to begin.
- For her lunch, Tricia had: a ham sandwich, an apple, a big salad and a yoghurt.

Introducing explanations
Colons are used to divide a sentence where the second part explains the first part. In other words, the second part of the sentence tells you more about the first part.
- *The bank was empty: everyone had finished work and gone home.*

Introducing dialogue in a script
Colons are used in dialogue. They appear after the person's name and before the words the person speaks.
- Cat: Lunch!
- Mouse: You'll be lucky…

Hint: Never use a semicolon to introduce a list.

Semicolons

You can use a semicolon: (a) **instead of a full stop or a conjunction** (b) **to break up lists** made up of longer phrases and (c) to **emphasise a contrast**.

Using semicolons instead of full stops or conjunctions

Semicolons can be used to turn two complete sentences into one. However, the two sentences must be about the same thing.

- *The boy tried his best in his geography test; he seemed determined to do well.*

In the example above, a **semicolon** is used instead of a full stop or a word like **but**.

Using semicolons to break up lists

Semicolons can be used to break up lists when the items in the list are long phrases.

- *The little kitten had round, green eyes; perfectly formed pink ears; curiously twitching whiskers; and a most playful look on her face.*

Using semicolons to emphasise a contrast

If you want to emphasise a contrast, you can use a semicolon.

- *Tricia passed the test with flying colours; Orla failed.*

Commas

A comma is used to mark a brief pause. The pause is much shorter than a pause made by a full stop. Below are some examples of when you need to use a comma.

> A comma should always help to make the meaning of a sentence clearer. If you use too many commas in a sentence, it makes it harder to read and understand. Only use them where you need them.

Using commas to separate items in a list

Commas are used to separate lists of words or phrases.
- *The ogre was huge, ugly, smelly and angry.*
- *The types of books I like are: adventure, science fiction, mystery and history.*
- *James did his project, watched some TV, tidied his room and then went to bed.*

The last two items in your list will be separated by the word **and**. You don't need to put a comma in before **and**.

Using commas in greetings
When you are writing letters, it is important to use commas after your greetings (when you are signing on and signing off).
- *Dear Hannah,*
- *Best wishes,*

Using commas around people's names in speech
- *'I was wondering, Jane, if you would like to come with me.'*
- *'Cathal, I'd like you to come and see my new puppy, Max.'*

Using commas to break up large numbers
You can break up large figures by using commas. Break the figure into units of three, starting from the right.
- *The winner received €5,000,000.*

Using commas when writing direct speech
- *'What I really feel like,' whispered Audrey, 'is a piece of chocolate.'*

Using commas after an introductory phrase in a sentence
The introduction words 'set the scene' of the sentence. The scene could be a time, a place or a fact.
- *As soon as the buns are golden brown, take them out of the oven.*

PUNCTUATION

Using commas before a conjunction

Words like **and**, **or** and **but** are known as conjunctions. Conjunctions can be used to join two sentences into one. When a conjunction is used in this way, it should have a comma before it.

- *She is a great swimmer, but she prefers to play tennis.*
- *The new teacher must be able to tell jokes and sing, and he must be able to dance.*

Using commas after an interjection

Expressions such as **yes**, **no** and **indeed** are known as **interjections**. Use a comma to separate them from the rest of the sentence.

- *Yes, she will apologise.*

Using commas to separate extra information

Commas can be used around pieces of extra information in a sentence. These extra words in the commas could be left out without changing the general meaning of the sentence.

- *Michael Landers, our star player, injured his leg in the match last Sunday.*

Using commas before question tags

- *'But I can't be ready to leave tomorrow evening, can I?'*

> **Hint**: You cannot join two sentences together with a comma alone. Try using a semicolon to join the two parts of the sentence – or write two separate sentences.

Inverted commas

We use **inverted commas** in direct speech. Inverted commas have many names. They are also called quotation marks, quotes or speech marks. Use them in your writing to show the *exact* words that someone has spoken.
- *'I can't wait for the summer!' said Cillian.*
- *The teacher said, 'You are not allowed to bring your skateboard to school.'*

Rules for using inverted commas in direct speech

You must use a **capital letter** whenever someone starts to speak.
- *Elaine asked Jennifer, 'What are you doing at the weekend?'*

Do **not** use a capital letter unless it either starts someone's spoken words or starts a sentence.
- *'Jennifer,' asked Elaine, 'what are you doing at the weekend?'*

When the words spoken come before the **saying verb** (says, said, etc.) and the words form a complete sentence, you must put a comma after them.
- *'I am very excited about going to the beach,' said Jennifer.*

If the words spoken are a question or an exclamation, use a question mark or an exclamation mark instead of a comma.
- *'When are you going?' asked Elaine.*

When the saying verb and the speaker appear at the start of the sentence, a comma is placed before the spoken words.
- *Jennifer replied, 'We are going on Saturday.'*

Other uses for inverted commas

When you use a short quote in your writing, put the spoken words in inverted commas.
- *My dad said that I was the 'best player in the world'.*

Inverted commas are used for the titles of short stories, poems and songs.
- *'Lipstick' is a song by Jedward.*

Inverted commas can add a funny twist to something you write. You can put them around certain words to show the reader that you do not take the meaning of these words seriously.
- *Our 'luxury' hotel turned out to be old barn with no heating!*

PUNCTUATION POEMS

These poems will help you to remember how to use all the different kinds of punctuation.

Ten Golden Rules of Punctuation
by Graham King

Sentences begin with a **capital letter**,
So as to make your writing better.

Use a **full stop** to mark the end.
It closes every sentence penned.

The **comma** is for short pauses and breaks,
And also for lists the writer makes.

Dashes – like these – are for thoughts by the way.
They give extra information (so do **brackets**, we may say).

These two dots are **colons**: they pause to compare.
They also do this: list, explain and prepare.

The **semicolon** makes a break; followed by a clause.
It does the job of words that link; it's also a short pause.

An **apostrophe** shows the owner of anyone's things,
And it's also useful for shortenings.

I'm so glad! He's so mad! We're having such a lark!
To show strong feelings use an **exclamation mark**!

A **question mark** follows: What? When? Where? Why? And How?
Do you? Can I? Shall we? Give us your answer now!

'**Quotation marks**' enclose what is said,
Which is why they're sometimes called 'speech marks' instead.

Punctuation Marks

The period is a busy man –
a small round traffic cop.
He blocks the helter-skelter words
and brings them to a stop.

The question mark's a tiny girl;
she's small but very wise.
She asks too many questions
for a person of her size.

Of all the punctuation folk,
I like the comma best.
For when I'm getting out of breath
he lets me take a rest.

Quotation marks are curious.
When friendly talk begins
you'll always find these little marks
are busy listening in.

The exclamation mark's an elf
whose easily excited.
When children laugh or cry or scream
it's then he's most delighted.

PUNCTUATION SUMMARY

The table below shows the different punctuation marks we use when writing. It explains what each one is called and it gives an example of how to use it.

Mark	Name	Example	Index
A B C	Capital letters	**J**ane, **A**bbie and **S**arah all played together after school.	see p.53
.	Full stop	The boys ran all the way home.	see p.55
?	Question mark	Where is my art picture?	see p.57
( )	Brackets	The streets were deserted (it was Christmas Day) and not a single shop was open.	see p.59
–	Dash	I opened the box carefully and inside there was – a mouse. (Here, the dash is used for effect.) He is a teacher – and a very good one too. (Here, the dash gives extra information.)	see p.59
!	Exclamation mark	Ouch!	see p.60

Mark	Name	Example	Index
-	Hyphen	We ate three-quarters of the pie.	see p.62
'	Apostrophe	Felix is Claire's cat. It's a sunny day.	see p.63
:	Colon	Here is what you must bring: togs, goggles, a towel and some lunch.	see p.66
;	Semicolon	She looked up at the sky; dark clouds suggested a storm.	see p.67
,	Comma	I bought pencils, pens, a ruler, a calculator and copy books.	see p.68
' '	Inverted commas	Hannah said, 'Please wait for us by the gate.'	see p.71

Hint: Read your writing aloud in your head to see if you have included all the necessary punctuation.

Writing:
Fiction and Non-fiction

PROCESS APPROACH TO WRITING

When you are writing, you must keep in mind the following stages:

1. Making decisions
2. Planning
3. Drafting
4. Responding, revising and proofreading
5. Presenting and publishing
6. Reflecting and setting targets

As you gain more confidence, you may decide that not all of these stages are necessary in your own writing.

1. Making decisions
Before you write you must decide the following:
- Topic: what do you want to write about?
- Audience: who is the writing for?
- Purpose: why are you writing the piece? (Is it to inform, explain, entertain, instruct, discuss, describe, recount or persuade?)
- Form: what type of writing will you use? (Is it report, narrative or something else?)

2. Planning
Planning means gathering together and ordering your ideas. You should:
- Brainstorm your ideas
- Organise and group your best ideas

- Make a rough plan/flow diagram
- Put your ideas in the correct order

> first
>
> then
>
> later
>
> after
>
> finally

3. Drafting

Writers often write drafts and redrafts of their writing. They add, delete and reorder their writing before they are happy with their finished work.

When writing your first draft and second draft:
- Write your revisions in the margins.
- Write on every second line so you will have space to add extra words or sentences later.
- Hunt for the right word or sentence, neatly crossing out a word or sentence and replacing it with a better or stronger word.
- Always cross out an idea or a word instead of rubbing it out: you may change your mind and want to use the first idea again later on.

First draft

Focus on your **ideas** from your brainstorm, thinking about the purpose, audience and form. Using these ideas, start writing your first draft with the help of a **writing frame**.

Check your draft by asking yourself these questions:
- Do I want to cross out or add an idea?
- Do I want to make changes that would improve my writing?
- Have I read my draft to another person (response partner) or group?

If you have read your draft to another person or group, take note of the ideas and suggestions they give you. You could ask them the following questions:
- Did you enjoy the writing? Why?
- Does it have a good beginning, middle and end?
- Did you understand everything?
- Did I leave out anything?
- Is everything in the right order?

> A writing frame is used as a *first draft* of a piece of writing. It is important that you cross things out and add things in at this stage. Discuss your completed writing frame (first draft) with a friend, a group or a teacher. This will help you to see if you need to make any more changes before you write your second draft.

Second draft

Once you have made changes to your first draft, then you are ready for the second draft. You need to check that your ideas are good and that they are written in the right order. You need to be certain that the meaning of your writing is clear. Once you are sure of all of this, you are ready to ask the following questions:
- Have I used the best words?
- Have I used a thesaurus?
- Do I have a mixture of long and short sentences?
- Have I used different sentences?
- Have I used connectives properly?

> You and your class can come up with a code of symbols to be used when writing drafts of your work. Try some of the following:
> - An eraser when something needs to be deleted
> - A magnifying glass when something needs to be changed or made clearer
> - A question mark when something has been left out
> - An arrow when text needs to be moved around
> - The letter P when punctuation needs to be checked
> - The letters SP when spelling needs to be checked

4. Responding, revising and proofreading

At this stage, your writing is nearly complete. You have discussed your piece of writing with others and you are now satisfied that all your ideas are written down clearly and in the correct order.

It is now time to proofread your work to make sure that everything is correct and clear: spelling, punctuation, grammar, facts, quotations and diagrams. You can use a dictionary or a computer spellcheck to help you with this. After proofreading, your text should have no mistakes and it should be easily read by others.

5. Presenting and publishing

After working hard on drafting and redrafting, it is now time to publish your work. If it's your own personal writing (like a diary), you may want to keep it to yourself! But if you decide that you are going to share it with an audience, you need to ask yourself the following questions:

- Will I use the computer or my own handwriting?
- Will I use pictures, photographs or illustrations?
- Will I share my writing in book form, on the school notice board or in the school magazine? Or will I read it aloud?

You can present or publish your writing in different formats.
- Narrative: e-book, short story or book
- Procedure: recipe book, poster or chart

- Information report: computer slideshow, poster or chart
- Recount: autobiography, journal or letter
- Explanation: computer slideshow, chart or poster
- Persuasion: speech, letter, email or advertisement
- Discussion: letter, email, interview, debate or conversation
- Response: review, feedback or assessment

6. Reflecting and setting targets

Before starting a new piece of writing, it is a good idea to look over the work you have just completed. Ask yourself the following questions:
- What was my writing about?
- How did I start?
- Where did I get my ideas?
- Did I change my ideas while writing?
- What did I find hard? What did I find easy? Why?
- How do I feel about the finished piece?
- Did I enjoy writing the piece?

It is also a good idea to talk to your teacher about your writing. Think about the things that you did really well and the things that you need to work on.

Try to set some targets so that you will improve in your next piece of writing.

WRITING FRAMES

In this section, we will examine different genres or types of writing. We will learn about: recount, narrative, report, procedure, explanation, persuasion, discussion and response texts.

There are templates or **writing frames** you can use. They will help you to write in the different genres. The writing frame will make sure that you remember all the parts that make up a particular genre.

When you are using a writing frame, you are working on a draft – in other words, your rough work. At this stage, you are trying to think of your ideas and how best to put these ideas into words. While you are working on your writing frame, you are allowed to cross out words and change them. You may want to cross out sentences or add new ones. The frame is only there to guide you.

All the best writers in the world write draft after draft until they are happy that their writing is interesting to read. If you want your writing to be interesting, you need to write a few drafts until you are satisfied.

WRITING: FICTION AND NON-FICTION

For your *first draft*, remember the *purpose* (why you are writing in the first place), the *audience* (who will be reading your writing) and the *form* (what text type you will use). Then think of all your ideas and what you want to say. At this stage, you can cross out words and ideas and change things around.

For your *second draft*, read through your first draft (aloud if possible). Now ask yourself if there is anything you need to add or change. Ask yourself if your ideas are in the right order.

At any stage of the writing process, read your work aloud to a person or group.

Now you are ready to *proofread* (check spelling, punctuation, etc.).

Once this is done, you are finally ready to publish your masterpiece!

FORMAL OR INFORMAL LANGUAGE?

When writing, it is important to think about your audience. These are the people who will be reading what you have written. Thinking about your audience will help you to decide what style of writing you should use. If your audience are young people or people you know (like your granny), you will use **informal** writing. Informal writing is chatty and it uses everyday language.

If you are writing to someone you don't know, you will use a more **formal** style of writing. Formal writing uses words and phrases that we don't necessarily use in everyday conversations. When you are writing in a formal style, think of yourself as an adult. Try to imagine how this person would say or write things. Do not use everyday expressions; instead, use **formal ways of saying things**. Instead of using **ask**, use **enquire**. Instead of using **put up with**, use **tolerate**.

In formal writing, you can use **technical words and phrases** related to the subject. If you are writing a report on recycling for a Green Flag project, you might use terms such as reusable, pollution or atmosphere.

Formal writing is usually **impersonal** and refers to groups of people in general and not individual people like you, me, him or her. It will say **people** or the **public** instead of **we** or **us.** Here is an example of this:
- *I think aliens will visit Earth. (personal)*

- *Some people believe aliens will visit Earth. (impersonal)*

> Your voice will sound chatty and informal in a letter or postcard to someone you know. On the other hand, your voice will sound formal and polite in a formal letter of complaint to someone you do not know, e.g. a restaurant owner.

LETTERS

People write letters for different reasons: to explain, to recount an event, to put across a point of view, to invite or to complain. Letters can be formal or informal.

Formal letters

Formal letters are usually written to:
- Make a complaint
- Request something
- Make an enquiry

Here is an example of a *formal* letter.

15 Main Street
Green Town
Co. Limerick

12 December 2013

Crowley's Fast Food
Old Town
Co. Tipperary

Dear Mr Crowley,

RE: Food, service and hygiene in your takeaway

  I wish to complain about the standard of food, service and hygiene in your fast-food takeaway. I saw a big crowd of people in your takeaway so I thought the food must be good – unfortunately that was not the case.
  Last Saturday, I went to your takeaway at about six o'clock. When I tried to give my order, the staff members were very rude. They were more interested in watching the soccer that was on the big screen in your takeaway than taking my order. Finally, when my order was taken, it took up to half an hour for me to get my food.
  When I got my food it was clear that the staff had given me the wrong order. To make matters worse, I noticed that the chicken was only half-cooked and the chips were soggy.

At this point, I refused to pay for the food and I asked to see the manager. While waiting for the manager to come to the counter, I had the dreadful experience of seeing a mouse scamper across the floor where the food was being prepared.

After waiting twenty minutes, I left without seeing the manager. I was told he was busy in the office. I left without the food (as it was inedible) and I have contacted the Health and Safety Authority to have your premises checked.

I hope that you will sort out these problems immediately so that no other customers should have to go through the same experience.

Yours sincerely,

Edel Walsh
Mrs Edel Walsh

Paragraphs in formal letters

The **introductory paragraph** should clearly state the purpose of the formal letter, e.g. making a complaint, making an enquiry or requesting something.

The **main body** of the formal letter should clearly state the points that you want to make. Stick to the point of your letter if you want to keep the reader interested.

The **concluding paragraph** of a formal letter should outline what action you would like the person to take, e.g. make a refund, send you information.

Here are my top tips for formal letters.

Top tips for formal letters

1. **Plan** your letter before you write it, thinking about what you want to say.
2. Write your address in the top **right-hand** corner, along with the date. Write the person's address on the **left-hand** side.
3. If you don't know the name of the person you are writing to, start your letter with **Dear Sir/Madam**.
4. In your **opening sentence**, say why you are writing the letter.

5. Use **formal language** in a formal letter. Instead of saying 'Please **write to Joe** O'Riordan,' say 'Please **contact Mr** O'Riordan'. **Avoid shortened words** (e.g. can't or won't) and **exclamation marks** – they are too informal for a formal letter.
6. Start a **new paragraph** for each new point you make.
7. If you are unsure of any **spellings**, check them in the dictionary. Use correct **punctuation**, e.g. full stops, commas and quotation marks.
8. Even if you are writing a letter of complaint, make sure your language is **polite** and your writing is **neat**.
9. If you started your letter with **Dear Sir/Madam**, end it with **Yours faithfully**. If you started your letter with the person's name, end it with **Yours sincerely**.
10. The formal letter writing frame will help you with this process.

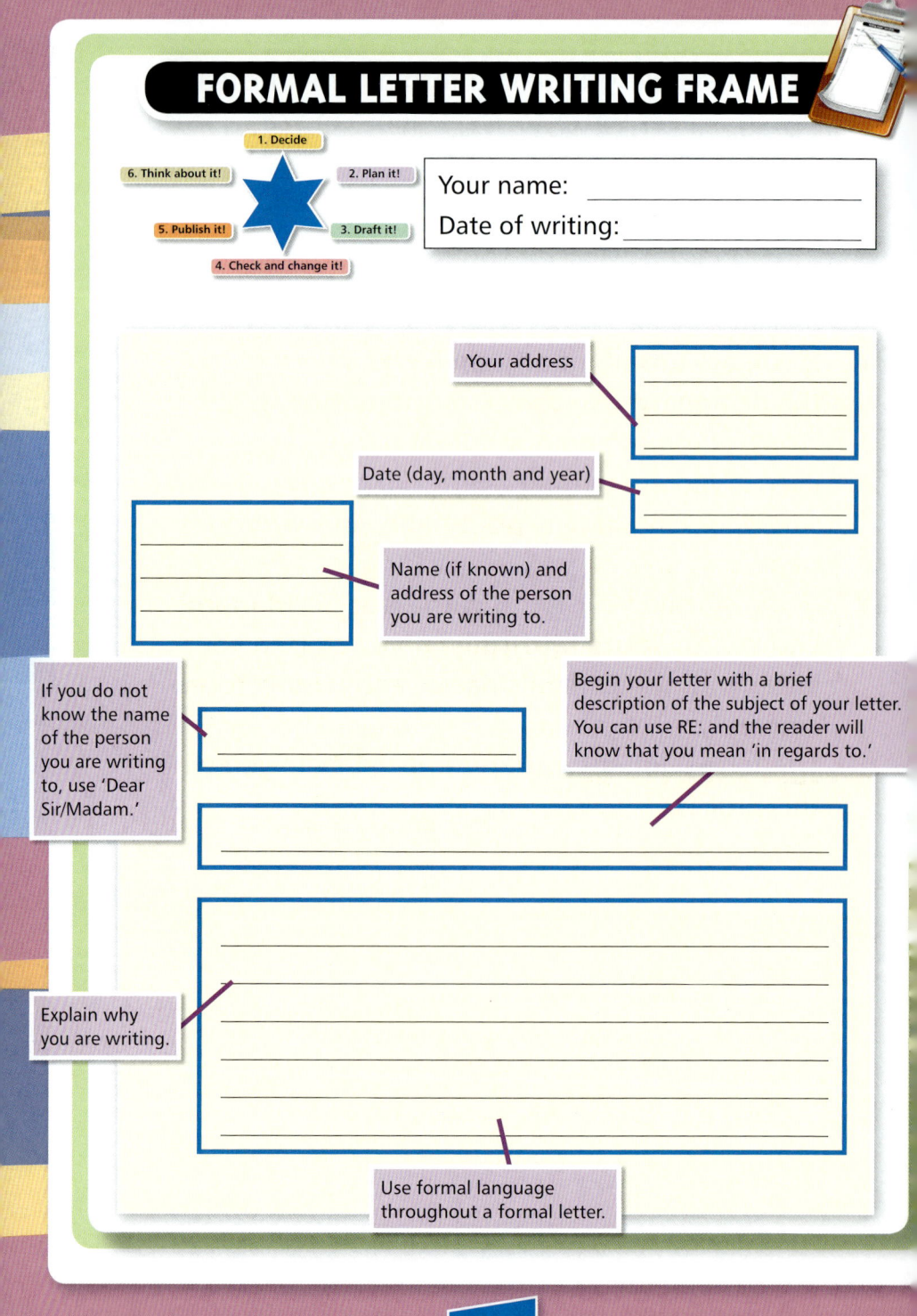

FORMAL LETTER WRITING FRAME

1. Decide
2. Plan it!
3. Draft it!
4. Check and change it!
5. Publish it!
6. Think about it!

Your name: _____
Date of writing: _____

Your address

Date (day, month and year)

Name (if known) and address of the person you are writing to.

If you do not know the name of the person you are writing to, use 'Dear Sir/Madam.'

Begin your letter with a brief description of the subject of your letter. You can use RE: and the reader will know that you mean 'in regards to.'

Explain why you are writing.

Use formal language throughout a formal letter.

WRITING: FICTION AND NON-FICTION

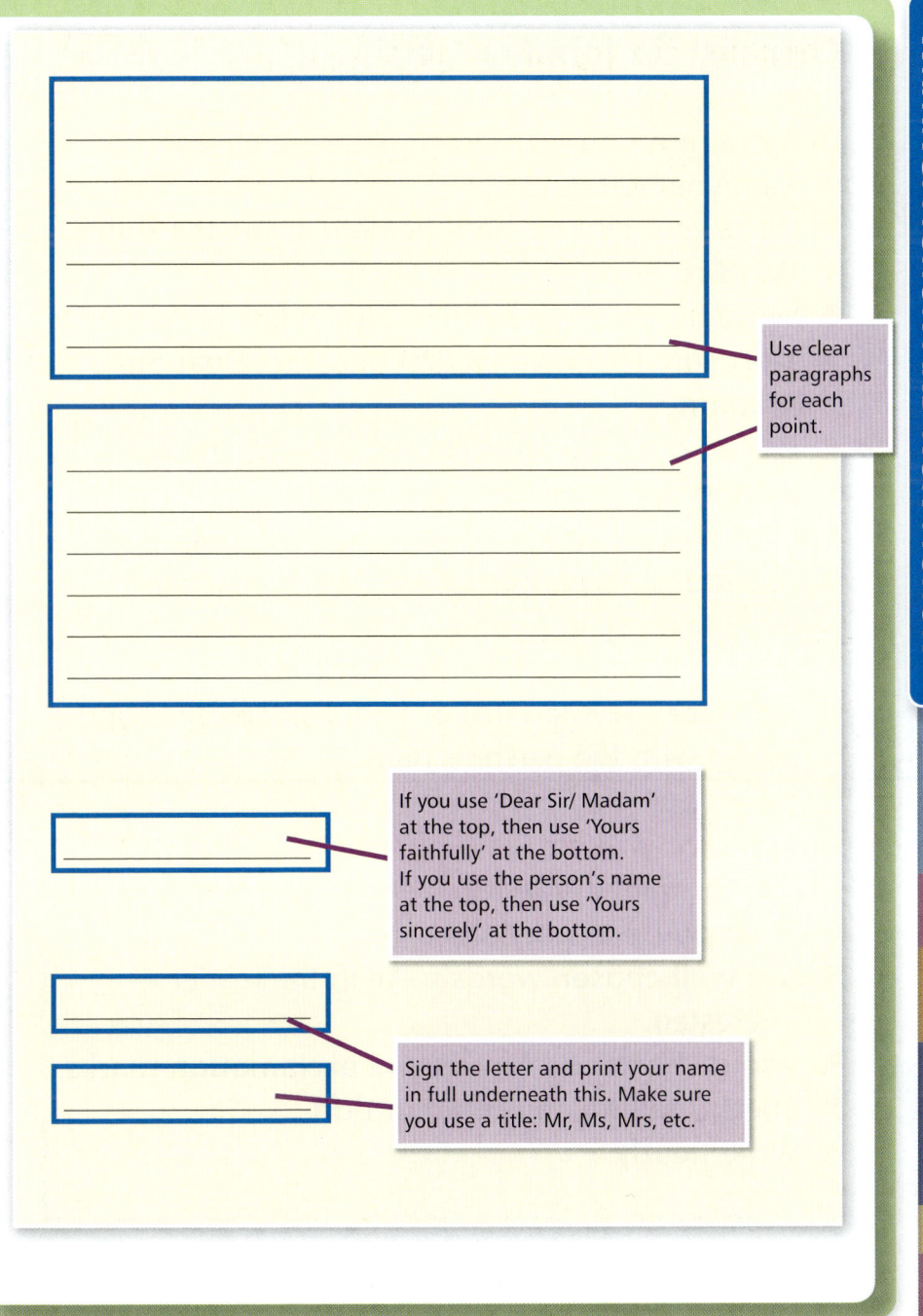

Use clear paragraphs for each point.

If you use 'Dear Sir/ Madam' at the top, then use 'Yours faithfully' at the bottom.
If you use the person's name at the top, then use 'Yours sincerely' at the bottom.

Sign the letter and print your name in full underneath this. Make sure you use a title: Mr, Ms, Mrs, etc.

Checklist for formal letters

Did you remember to do all of these things?
- **Plan** your letter.
- Write your address and the date in the top **right-hand** corner.
- Write the person's address on the **left-hand** side.
- Start your letter with a greeting, e.g. **Dear Sir/Madam**.
- Use an **opening sentence** to say why you are writing the letter.
- Start a **new paragraph** for each new point.
- Use a **closing paragraph** to say what action you want taken, e.g. refund.
- End your letter with **Yours faithfully** (if you began with **Dear Sir/Madam**) or **Yours sincerely** (if you began with the person's name).

Did you show the following writing skills?
- Use **formal language**.
- Be as **polite** as possible.
- Use **well-chosen** words to keep the reader interested.
- **Avoid shortened words** and **exclamation marks**.
- Check **spelling** and **punctuation**.
- Write **neatly**.

Informal letters

Informal letters are usually written to:
- Express congratulations
- Exchange news
- Communicate with friends
- Apologise for doing something wrong
- Catch up with family members who live far away
- Express thanks
- Show appreciation

Here is an example of an *informal* letter.

Cherry Tree Lane
Ballincollig
Co. Cork

15 November 2013

Dear Granny,

    I hope you are well. Thank you for writing to tell me about your weekend in Dublin. It sounds like you and Granddad had an amazing time. We also had a great time on holiday in Spain, but you'll never believe what happened to us – we had two airport disasters!

    You'll remember that we were supposed to be going to Barcelona. Well, we had everything ready the night before and we got up really early to go to the airport the next morning. All of us were really tired. On the way to the airport, I suddenly remembered that we left Fifi home alone!

    Can you believe it? We had to turn around and go right back! When we got back, Fifi was fast asleep and snoring in Mum and Dad's bed! She looked like she was happy to have the house to herself. By the time we dropped Fifi off to the kennels and raced back to the airport we had missed our flight. We had to wait five hours to get on the next flight to Barcelona. It was really boring sitting in the airport! The good thing is that we had an amazing time in Spain and the weather was fab!

At the end of the week, we didn't want to leave and I was feeling a bit sad on the way to the airport. Then we had our second airport disaster! We were all on the plane when we felt a thud! The truck that refuels the plane had backed into the plane's wing and damaged it. We had to sit on the plane for two hours while the wing was being fixed and it was so boring! Dad tried to entertain us, but it didn't work as we all wanted to be back at the hotel, swimming in the pool! Eventually the pilot said the plane was in 'ship shape' and we took off. It was midnight when we arrived back and everyone was tired but glad to be home.

I hope you and Granddad will visit soon so I can show you the photographs.

Lots of love,

Seán

Here are my top tips for informal letters.

Top tips for informal letters

1. **Plan** your letter before you write it, thinking about what you want to say.
2. Write your address in the **top right-hand** corner, along with the date.
3. Use a **greeting**, e.g. Dear Granny.
4. Use chatty, **everyday language** in an informal letter. You can use shortened words (e.g. can't or won't) and exclamation marks. Try to keep the reader interested by using **well-chosen words**. A thesaurus might help you here.
5. Start a **new paragraph** for each new point you make.
6. If you are unsure of any **spellings**, check them in the dictionary. Use correct **punctuation**, e.g. full stops, commas and quotation marks.
7. Even though your letter is informal and relaxed, make sure your language is **polite** and your writing is neat.
8. Your letter should end with a concluding paragraph that sums up your letter in a friendly way.
9. Finish your letter with a friendly goodbye (e.g. **All my love**) and then sign your name.
10. The informal letter writing frame will help you with this process.

INFORMAL LETTER WRITING FRAME

1. Decide
2. Plan it!
3. Draft it!
4. Check and change it!
5. Publish it!
6. Think about it!

Your name: _____
Date of writing: _____

Your address

Start with 'Dear…' and use their first name.

Date (day, month and year)

Use the first sentence to ask how they are and give the reason for your letter.

Clear paragraphs for each point

End your letter in a friendly way. Don't use 'Yours Sincerely', as this is for formal letters only.

The concluding paragraph sums up the letter in a friendly way.

Just sign your first name.

WRITING: FICTION AND NON-FICTION

Checklist for informal letters

Did you remember to do all of these things?
- **Plan** your letter.
- Write your address and the date in the top **right-hand** corner.
- Start your letter with a **greeting**, e.g. Dear Granny.
- Start a **new paragraph** for each new point.
- **Sum up** your letter in the last paragraph.
- End with a **friendly goodbye**, e.g. All my love.

Did you show the following writing skills?
- Use **informal language**.
- Be as **polite** as possible.
- Use **well-chosen words** to keep the reader interested.
- Check **spelling** and **punctuation**.
- Write **neatly**.

Addressing envelopes

When you write a formal or an informal letter, you will need to address the envelope.

The address can be written in a few different ways. You can keep each line to the **left**:

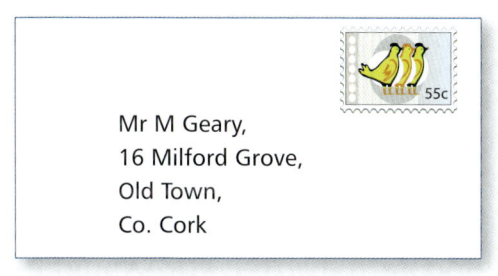

> Mr M Geary,
> 16 Milford Grove,
> Old Town,
> Co. Cork

Or you can arrange the lines like **steps**:

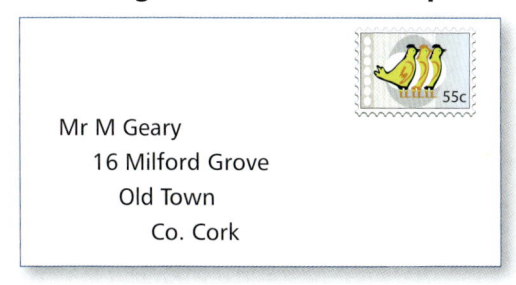

> Mr M Geary
>   16 Milford Grove
>   Old Town
>   Co. Cork

You can use commas at the ends of the lines – except for the last line. The **first version** (above) shows this.

You can also write the address **without** any punctuation at the ends of the lines. The **second version** (above) shows this.

Some addresses have postcodes (e.g. Dublin 1). If the address has a postcode, this will appear in the bottom line of the address.

Emails

Along with letters, people also use emails, text messages and social networking sites to keep in touch with each other.

An email is just a letter typed and sent on your computer. We write emails for the same reasons we write letters: to say thank you, to request information, to complain or to give information.

Emails are faster than letters and they allow you to attach photos or scanned pictures. If you were sending some photos along with a letter, you would have to print them off first.

Like letters, there are **formal** and **informal** emails.

> You can use the same tips for letter-writing when you want to write an email. If your email is formal, follow the tips for formal letters. If your email is informal, follow the tips for informal letters.

EMAIL WRITING FRAME

1. Decide
2. Plan it!
3. Draft it!
4. Check and change it!
5. Publish it!
6. Think about it!

Your name: _____
Date of writing: _____

Head

To: Type the person's email address here
Subject: Type the topic of your email here

Greeting

Dear (formal email)

or

Hi (informal email)

Message

Your message can be broken into sections:

Introduction	Introduce yourself/say why you are sending the email
Main body	Put your main message across
Personal comments	Conclude with personal comments/actions you want taken if this is a formal email

Conclusion

Regards or **Yours sincerely**   (formal email)
[Your full name and address]

All my love or **See you soon**   (informal email)
[Your first name only]

> Like letters, emails should be polite. Your computer spellcheck will help you with spelling mistakes but you should still read your email carefully and check for spelling and punctuation before you send it.

WRITING: FICTION AND NON-FICTION

RECOUNT

Recount writing comes in many different **forms**, including: biographies, autobiographies, diaries, newspaper reports, letters and eyewitness accounts of incidents.

A **personal recount** is used when you are retelling your own personal experience, e.g. your visit to the beach. A **factual recount** is used to retell a **known** event or incident, e.g. an accident.

Purpose of recount

The purpose of recount writing is to **retell an event** so that the reader knows:
- **When** the event happened
- **Where** it happened
- **Who** was there
- **What** happened
- **Why** it happened.

The writer often gives their personal opinion on what is being recounted.

Audience for recount

You could be writing for different types of audiences, e.g. a close friend or the entire country. If you are writing a diary, **you** will be your own audience!

Usually, you are writing a recount for someone who wasn't there when the event happened, but they need to know all about it.

Forms of recount

Recount writing has many forms, including:

> travel journals   diaries   newspaper articles
> letters   emails   history books
> eyewitness accounts   biographies
> autobiographies   postcards

Here is an example of recount writing. It was written by June Crebbin, who was recounting her first day back at school after the summer holidays.

First Day Back
by June Crebbin

It seems to me since time began,
it seems to be the rule
that every teacher has to say,
first day back at school:

'What did you do in the holidays?
Write as much as you can.
Did you travel abroad this year
or stay in a caravan?

WRITING: FICTION AND NON-FICTION

'Did you visit a stately home
or walk in the countryside?
Remember to put in the details
so that I know you've tried.

'Perhaps you went to the seaside;
perhaps you stayed with Gran.
We'll call it "Holiday Memories" – now
write as much as you can.'

Same old thing, year in year out,
and everybody knows
we'll have to write at least a page.
Oh well, eyes down, here goes...

> Here is another example of *recount writing*. It was written by Abby O'Doherty, who was recounting her Spanish holiday.

Mind map

Who will read this piece of writing? **My teddy bear Snowy and me**

The type of recount piece I am going to write... **Diary entry**

The Ws (who, when, why, where)...

Myself, my family and my friend's family

In Spain

In the summer because it looked like so much fun

Finally... **In the airport people were staring at me, but I felt fine**

The event I am going to write about... **My Spanish boating accident**

After that... **He said to my brother 'It's your turn now!' My brother was very mad at him. I said 'Let's go back now!'**

Then... **My friend and I put our life jackets on and they strapped us on.**

First main event **I got on the boat and we roared across the Spanish ocean**

He said 'One, two, three.'
Disaster!
Cut cheek and a bruised chin.

WRITING: FICTION AND NON-FICTION

Abby's Recount Writing Frame

RECOUNT WRITING FRAME

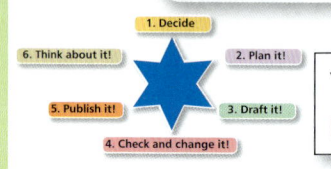

1. Decide
2. Plan it!
3. Draft it!
4. Check and change it!
5. Publish it!
6. Think about it!

Your name: __Abby O'Doherty__
Date of writing: __01/03/13__

Title My Spanish Holiday

Introduction

WHO	Who was there?	Myself, my family and my friend Nicola's family
WHEN	When did it happen?	In the summer
WHERE	Where did it happen?	In Spain
WHY	Why did it happen?	Because it looked like so much fun

Main events (**What** happened?)

Recount the main events in the **order** in which they happened.

FIRST	We got on the boat and we roared across the Spanish ocean.
THEN	He strapped Nicola and me in (we had our life jackets on).
LATER	He said 'One, two, three,' but oh no! The parachute fell and it pulled Nicola and me off the boat and into the ocean.
AFTER	I had a bruised chin and a cut cheek. Poor Nicola got a bump on her head.
FINALLY	My mum got the fright of her life.

Conclusion

What did you **think**, **feel** or **decide** about the events that happened?

One thing is for sure: I will never go paragliding again.

First draft

Dear Diary,

I have had quite a summer! ~~I am writing about~~ Maybe the biggest event was my Spanish boating accident! It was ~~very~~ extremely scary! Here I go:

   It was another beautiful day in Spain, so we decided to go paragliding. I had never been before and was very excited – but if I knew then what I know now, I don't think I would have gone! My brother and I had a little argument about who ~~went~~ would go first: ~~him~~ he and his friend, or me and mine. Nicola and I got to go first.

   We jumped on the boat and it roared across the Spanish ocean. The captain played some really loud music from the boat and he strapped us into our harnesses, which held the parachutes on them. (Of course, we were wearing our life jackets.) But…he forgot to tie Nicola's harness! All of a sudden the parachute fell down and it whipped both of us off the boat!

   We both tumbled off ~~the boat~~ and into the water. We were so frightened. Nicola saw that I had a cut and it was bleeding, so we were extra scared that a shark might smell the blood and attack us! We wanted to be rescued but the boat kept going!

   Eventually, the captain turned around and got us on board the boat. I was so dizzy. We were brought straight to the SOS tent on the beach. It was such a scary experience and, after all that, can you believe that the captain asked my brother if he wanted a go? Luckily this experience did not ruin my holiday completely, especially since it was the last day. It would have been much worse if it was the first day. Tomorrow, I'm going to write about my flight back to Ireland.

Final version

Recount

| Abby O'Doherty Third Class | St Raphaela's NS Co. Dublin | 'My Spanish Holiday' |

Dear Diary,

   I have had quite a summer! Maybe the biggest event was my Spanish boating accident! It was extremely scary! Here I go:
It was another beautiful day in Spain, so we decided to go paragliding. I had never been before and was very excited – but if I knew then what I know now, I don't think I would have gone! My brother and I had a little argument about who would go first: he and his friend, or me and mine. Nicola and I got to go first.

   We jumped on the boat and it roared across the Spanish ocean. The captain played some really loud music from the boat and he strapped us into our harnesses, which held the parachutes on them. (Of course, we were wearing our life jackets.) But...he forgot to tie Nicola's harness! All of a sudden the parachute fell down and it whipped both of us off the boat.

   We both tumbled off and into the water. We were so frightened. Nicola saw that I had a cut and it was bleeding, so we were extra scared that a shark might smell the blood and attack us! We wanted to be rescued but the boat kept going!

   Eventually, the captain turned around and got us on board the boat. I was so dizzy. We were brought straight to the SOS tent on the beach. It was such a scary experience and, after all that, can you believe that the captain asked my brother if he wanted a go? Luckily this experience did not ruin my holiday completely, especially since it was the last day. It would have been much worse if it was the first day. Tomorrow, I'm going to write about my flight back to Ireland.

Top tips for recount
1. Use the mind map on p.107 to help you to **brainstorm** your recount.

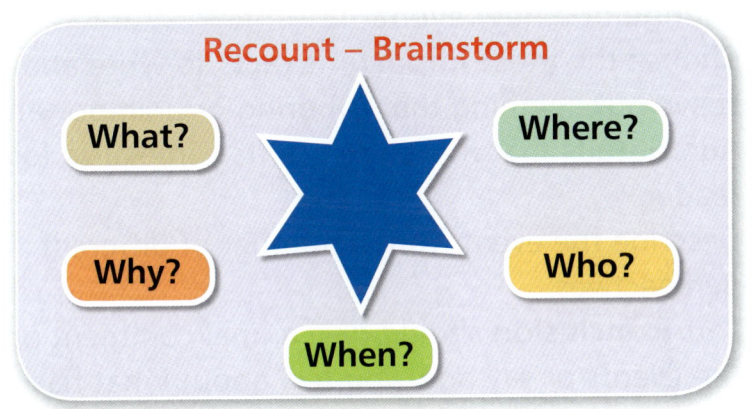

Recount – Brainstorm
- What?
- Where?
- Why?
- Who?
- When?

2. After brainstorming, record the events in the correct **order**.

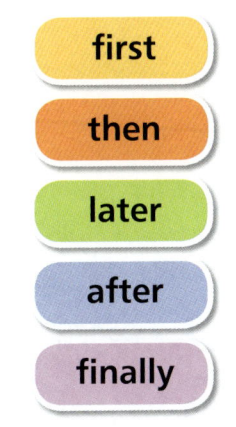

- first
- then
- later
- after
- finally

3. Write an **introduction** that sets the scene. Give important background information about **who**, **when**, **where** and **why**.
4. Write in the **past tense** and use the **first** or **third** person narrative.

5. Recount the **main events** (**what** happened) in the order in which they happened.
6. Start a **new paragraph** when there is a **time change** or a **new event**.
7. Choose the **most important facts** to write about. Leave out anything that is boring or unimportant. Add **details** that make the events come alive for the reader.
8. Describe the event from a number of different perspectives.
9. Your **conclusion** should give a final comment on the events or say how you feel about what has happened.
10. The recount writing frame will help you with this process.

Don't put conversations in – just describe what people said (indirect speech).

RECOUNT WRITING FRAME

1. Decide
2. Plan it!
3. Draft it!
4. Check and change it!
5. Publish it!
6. Think about it!

Your name: _____
Date of writing: _____

WRITING: FICTION AND NON-FICTION

Title: The title of your piece

Introduction

Set the scene by giving **background information** on:

WHO — Who was there?
_____
_____

WHEN — When did it happen?
_____
_____

WHERE — Where did it happen?
_____
_____

WHY — Why did it happen?
_____
_____

Main events (**What** happened?)

Recount the main events in the **order** in which they happened.

FIRST
_____
_____
_____
_____
_____

THEN

LATER

AFTER

FINALLY

Conclusion

What did you **think**, **feel** or **decide** about the events that happened?

Checklist for recount

Did you remember to do all of these things?
- Write an interesting **title** for your piece.
- **Brainstorm** your recount.
- Give background information on **who**, **when**, **where** and **why**.
- Recount the main events in the **order** in which they happened.
- Write about the **important** facts, leaving out anything unimportant.
- **Conclude** with what you thought, felt or decided about the event.

Did you show the following writing skills?
- Use **time connectives**: next, meanwhile, after, etc.
- Use the **past tense**.
- Write in **first** or **third** person narrative.
- Add **detail** to make your recount come alive.
- Start a **new paragraph** for each time change or new event.
- **Comment** on the event.
- Check **spelling** and **punctuation**.
- Write **neatly**.

Newspaper Reports

The purpose of a newspaper report is to inform the public of current events. Newspaper reports are similar to recounts in that they describe what happened. However, newspaper reports have some special features of their own.

Here is an example of the layout of a newspaper report.

HEADLINE	THE HEADLINE IS A STATEMENT THAT GRABS THE READER'S ATTENTION! Headlines are like short poems: they communicate a lot of information in a small amount of space. Therefore, the words must be chosen carefully. A good idea is to use alliteration.
BY-LINE	The by-line gives the name of the journalist.
LEAD	The lead is the first paragraph. It is usually only one or two lines long. The lead sets the scene and summarises the main facts of the report: who, what, where, when and why. The lead must also contain a hook: something that grabs the reader's attention and makes them want to read the full report.
BODY	The body of the article contains supporting paragraphs that go into more detail about the topic or event. Quotes and interesting facts can be used, but the reporter should keep their personal opinions out of the report. The language must be clear and easily understood. The report should be concise and factually correct.
FINAL COMMENT	A final comment can appear at the end of the article. This sums up the events or anticipates what might happen next.

> Here is an example of a *newspaper report*. It was written by Clodagh Walsh.

Newspaper Report

| Clodagh Walsh Sixth Class | Tullylease NS Co. Cork | 'Golf Balls Galore' |

GOLF BALLS GALORE

Yesterday morning the people of Tullylease were woken by loud banging on their windows and roofs. On further investigation they were amazed to find the banging was caused by golf balls falling from the sky.

Tullylease is a small village in north Cork near the Limerick border. It has a population of around 350 people. Everyone in the area is devastated by the damage caused. The golf balls hit cars, broke windows and even injured people. Several people were taken to Cork University Hospital by ambulance.

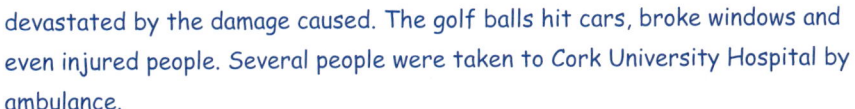

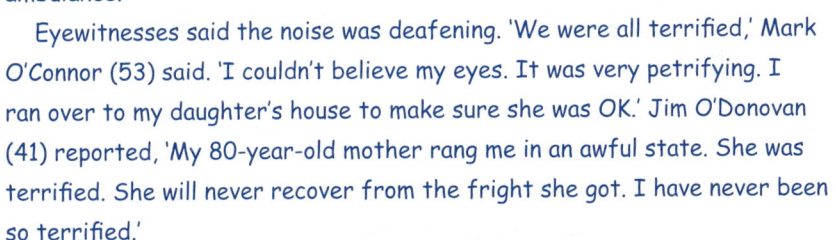

Eyewitnesses said the noise was deafening. 'We were all terrified,' Mark O'Connor (53) said. 'I couldn't believe my eyes. It was very petrifying. I ran over to my daughter's house to make sure she was OK.' Jim O'Donovan (41) reported, 'My 80-year-old mother rang me in an awful state. She was terrified. She will never recover from the fright she got. I have never been so terrified.'

No explanation has yet been given but investigations are ongoing. Experts believe that a freak hurricane over a golf course in Scotland (St Andrews Links) vacuumed all the golf balls, brought them across the Irish Sea and dropped them here in Tullylease. Events like this are extremely unique. The people of Tullylease hope it will never happen again.

The government is holding an emergency meeting next Thursday to discuss the situation. They will formulate a plan on how to act if this should ever occur again.

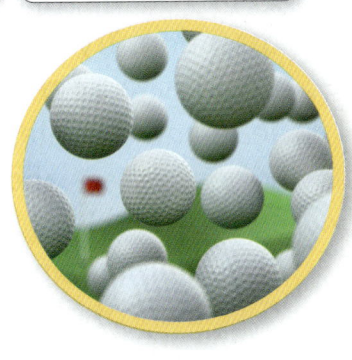

WRITING: FICTION AND NON-FICTION

> Here are my top tips for newspaper reports.

Top tips for newspaper reports

1. **Research** the topic of your article.
2. Start with a **headline** that will grab the reader's attention. Try to sound dramatic or amusing.
3. Begin with an **overview** of events. This is called the **lead** and it contains information about **who**, **what**, **when**, **where** and **why**.
4. In the main body of the text, you should **explain the headline** and the **lead**.
5. Give a **chronological** account of the main events. Use **separate paragraphs** to make each event clear.
6. Give **precise information** about the people involved in the story.
7. Include **quotes** from the people involved or the people who saw the events (eyewitnesses). You can use direct or indirect speech.
8. Use **exciting words** to keep your reader interested.
9. At the end of the report, give a **final comment** that sums up the events or anticipates what might happen next.
10. The newspaper report writing frame will help you with this process.

NEWSPAPER REPORT WRITING FRAME

1. Decide
2. Plan it!
3. Draft it!
4. Check and change it!
5. Publish it!
6. Think about it!

Your name: _____
Date of writing: _____

Headline (4–5 words)

By-line

Photo

Lead
- Who?
- What?
- When?
- Where?
- Why?

Hook

Paragraph 1
Write about the most important point of the report.
Describe exactly what happened and why.

Paragraph 2
Write about the second most important point here – and so on.

Conclusion
Give a final comment that sums up the main events or anticipates what might happen next.

Use **quotes** in your report. Make sure that you quote the speaker accurately and identify who said what!

WRITING: FICTION AND NON-FICTION

Checklist for newspaper reports

Did you remember to do all of these things?
- **Create a headline** with attention-grabbing words.
- Include a **by-line** with your name on it.
- Provide a **photo** that is linked to the report.
- Write the **lead**, summarising **who**, **what**, **where**, **when** and **why**.
- Include a **hook**.
- Write about the most important point in the **first** paragraph.
- Write an explanation in the **main body**, giving additional information.
- Use **quotes**.
- Give a final **comment** that sums up the main events or anticipates what might happen next.

Did you show the following writing skills?
- Use **short sentences** and **clear language**.
- Start a **new paragraph** for each new point.
- Check **spelling** and **punctuation**.
- Write **neatly**.

> Recount writing also includes biographies and diary entries. You can learn about all of these things by visiting our website: www.gillmacmillan.ie/primary

PROCEDURE

Procedure writing involves writing instructions. Instructions are written to tell the reader **how** to do something, e.g. how to make something, how to get somewhere or how to play a game. Sometimes pictures are used along with the instructions.

Before writing instructions, you should think through the activity and break it up into clear and easy steps.

Purpose of procedure
The purpose of procedure writing is to explain to the reader how to do something, e.g. instructions for playing an online game.

Audience for procedure
Your audience is someone who wants to know how to make something or do something. You need to keep in mind the age of your audience – and tailor your instructions to suit them.

Forms of procedure
Procedure writing is all around us. It comes in many forms, including:

cookbooks   games   assembly kits   posters   charts
manuals   instructions   science books   experiments

Here is an example of *procedure writing*. It is a recipe for cupcakes, written by Nadine Goodison.

How to make cupcakes

- oven
- blender
- tray
- cases
- eggs/other food
- weighing scale
- whisk
- food colouring
- spoons
- chocolate chips
- icing sugar
- bowl
- decorations

Nadine's procedure writing frame

PROCEDURE WRITING FRAME

1. Decide
2. Plan it!
3. Draft it!
4. Check and change it!
5. Publish it!
6. Think about it!

Your name: Nadine Goodison
Date of writing: 05/03/13

Title: Cupcakes

Aim/goal: Make a batch of 12 cupcakes

Items/equipment: Tray, cases, weighing scale, spoon, bowl, whisk, decorations, chocolate chips, icing sugar, eggs/other food, food colouring, blender, oven

Drawing/photos:

Method:
1. Take out your materials and put the cases into the tray.
2. Measure the flour (175g), sugar (125g) and margarine (125g) in your weighing scale.
3. Crack the eggs into a cup.
4. Pour the stuff into a bowl.
5. Turn on your whisk and blend them.
6. When they are mixed get your spoon and scoop and pat them into the cases and put them into the oven for 15 minutes.
7. Decorate your buns with chocolate chips and icing.
8. Enjoy!

WRITING: FICTION AND NON-FICTION

Warning: If you are cooking or baking, there must be an adult present.

Final version

Procedure

| Nadine Goodison Fourth Class | Scoil Mhuire Co. Wexford | 'Recipe for cupcakes' |

Title: Cupcakes
Aim: To make a batch of 12 cupcakes

Materials
- oven
- weighing scales
- muffin tin
- 12 x muffin cases
- large mixing bowl
- handheld electric whisk
- cup
- fork
- spoon
- oven gloves
- wire rack
- sieve
- small mixing bowl
- knife

Ingredients
- 125g margarine
- 125g caster sugar
- 2 eggs
- 1 teaspoon vanilla extract
- 175g self-raising flour
- 1 tablespoon milk

For the icing
- 150g icing sugar
- 1 tablespoon water
- 2 drops food colouring
- chocolate chips or other decorations

Method
1. Wash your hands.
2. Preheat the oven to 180°C/350°F/Gas 4.
3. Weigh out all the ingredients.
4. Line the tin with muffin cases.
5. Place the margarine and sugar in the large mixing bowl. Use the whisk to blend them together.
6. Crack the eggs into the cup and beat lightly with the fork.
7. Add the egg to the margarine and sugar mixture, a little at a time, whisking after each addition.
8. Stir in the vanilla extract.
9. Fold in the flour.
10. Stir in the milk.
11. Spoon the mixture into the paper cases.
12. With the help of an adult, place the tray in the oven.
13. Bake the cupcakes for 8–15 minutes, until golden brown on top.
14. Use oven gloves to remove the tray from the oven. Set aside for 10 minutes to cool.
15. Remove the cupcakes from the tin and leave them to cool fully on the wire rack.
16. While the cupcakes are cooling, make the icing. Sift the icing sugar into the small mixing bowl.
17. Stir in enough water to create a smooth mixture, then stir in the food colouring.
18. To ice the cupcakes, drizzle the icing on top and sprinkle with chocolate chips or other decorations.
19. Set aside until the icing hardens.
20. When the cupcakes are ready, share them with your family and friends!

Here are my top tips for procedure writing.

Top tips for procedure

1. Choose a **title** (Cupcakes) and **aim** (to make a batch of 12 cupcakes) to introduce the instructions, e.g. recipe for cupcakes.
2. List any **items or equipment** needed.
3. Write a clear **step-by-step method** for completing the task. Put the verb as close to be beginning of each step as you can.
4. Use **short sentences** (commands) where possible.
5. Add **important details** by using well-chosen adjectives and adverbs.
6. Use language that is **easy** to follow.
7. **Number** each step of the procedure. Write a new instruction for each different **stage** of the task.
8. Give the reader any necessary details about **how**, **when** and **where** things should be done.
9. Include a final statement at the end of the method, e.g. sit back and enjoy your Rice Krispie buns! (Do not do this when writing a science experiment.)
10. The procedure writing frame will help you with this process.

Good instructions will make even a difficult task seem easy! The trick is to break everything down into clear, easy-to-follow steps. During the writing process, read your instructions to a friend or group. They will be able to tell you whether or not the instructions are clear.

PROCEDURE WRITING FRAME

1. Decide
2. Plan it!
3. Draft it!
4. Check and change it!
5. Publish it!
6. Think about it!

Your name: _____
Date of writing: _____

Title Choose a title that explains the aim of the instructions.

Aim/goal Say what will be made or done.

Items/equipment List any items or equipment that will be needed.

Drawing/photos Include a drawing of the procedure if it will be helpful for the reader.

Method
1. Give step-by-step instructions for carrying out the procedure.
2. Number the instructions.
3. Give a new instruction for each stage of the task.
4. The final instruction should be a statement that sums up what happens when all the instructions have been completed.

Checklist for procedure

Did you remember to do all of these things?
- Choose a **title** and **goal/aim** to introduce your instructions.
- List the **items and equipment** needed.
- Include any **drawings or photographs** that might help the reader to understand the instructions.
- Write a **step-by-step method**.
- **Number** the instructions.
- Start a new instruction for each stage of the task.
- Give a **final instruction** that sums up what the outcome should be.

Did you show the following writing skills?
- Write only the **necessary** details.
- Use **connective words** to help explain the method: **first**, **then**, **now**, etc.
- Use clear **commands**: **mix**, **stir**, **lift**, **sieve**, etc.
- Check **spelling** and **punctuation**.
- Write **neatly**.

INFORMATION REPORTS

Purpose of information reports
The purpose of an information report is to describe and give information about something in an organised way.

An information report gives the reader information about **people**, **animals**, **objects** or **places**.

Seahorses make clicking sounds when eating.

Audience for information reports
Your audience is anyone looking for information on a given topic. You must keep in mind the age of your audience, since this will affect the way you write and present your report, e.g. when writing for a Junior Infant child, use simple words and colourful pictures.

Forms of information reports
Information reports have many forms, including:

> non-fiction books   encyclopaedias
> magazine articles   presentations   brochures

Writing an information report
Sometimes when we write, we are telling people about something or giving information. This is called **non-fiction** writing. A report is an example of non-fiction writing. Reports are used to give factual information, which means that you need **true facts**. Reports often include definitions, descriptions and factual information about something.

Here is an example of an *information report*. It was written by Cáit Healy on the topic of 'Tigers'.

Information Report

Cáit Healy
Fourth Class

Gaelscoil Charraig na Siúire
Co. Thiobraid Árann

'Tigers'

Tigers are the world's largest cats, growing up to 3.3 metres and weighing up to 306 kilograms. The smallest tiger was a female Sumatran tiger, who grew to 230 centimetres.

There are six types of tiger:

Siberian or Amur Tiger — The largest tiger – males can be as long as a station wagon.

Bengal or Indian Tiger — The most common tiger – as its name suggests, it is found all over India.

Indochinese Tiger — These tigers are about 20 per cent smaller and are darker in colour than their Bengal cousin.

Malaysian Tiger — This type of tiger was proven to be a 'true subspecies', living in Thailand and Malaysia in 2004.

South China Tiger — In the 1950s, the Chinese government ordered that these tigers be destroyed, since they were viewed as pests. There are as few as 30 wild South China tigers left.

Sumatran Tiger — Even though the Sumatran is one of the smallest types of tiger, it's still pretty big – it is the length of a table!

Tigers once lived all across Asia, from west Turkey to the eastern coast of Russia.

All tigers are carnivores, so they usually eat meat. Depending on where they live, they can eat antelope, deer, boars and yaks as well as much smaller prey such as hares, monkeys and wild dogs.

A tiger's worst enemy is a poacher. Tiger poaching is illegal but people still hunt them because tiger fur is very valuable and tiger body parts are used for medicine.

There are fewer than 100,000 tigers left in the world, so everybody should help to protect these furry felines.

Here are my top tips for information reports.

Top tips for information reports
Preparation and planning
1. Get to know all about your topic. **Research** all the facts using the internet, newspapers and books.
2. As you read about your topic, **take notes** on key information that you will use in your report.
3. Once you have gathered all your information, **sort it** under different headings.
4. Write formally or use impersonal language – for example, you cannot say *I love polar bears*.

Introduction
5. Start with a short **introduction**, which can include:
   - A statement that tells the audience what the text will be about
   - A short description of the topic
   - A definition of the topic

Body of the report
6. In the body of the report, all the main information about the topic is broken into headings and paragraphs.
7. Each paragraph starts with a **topic sentence**. Each paragraph gives information about **one** part of the topic.
8. Paragraphs may include **technical language**, so you can add a **glossary** to your report.

9. Include facts only when you are certain they are **true**, e.g. *Seahorses are the slowest fish in the ocean. They do not have scales like other fish; they have skin.*
10. **Do not** start every sentence with the name of your topic, e.g. *Seahorses have a head like a horse. Seahorses have a tail like a monkey. Seahorses are really a fish.*
11. Vary your sentences by using pronouns, e.g. *It has a head like a horse and a tail like a monkey, but the seahorse is really a fish.*
12. Use a mixture of **simple and compound sentences**, e.g. *Seahorses are weak swimmers* (simple sentence). *They wrap their curly tails around plants and this prevents them from being dragged away by the water* (compound sentence).
13. Use the **present tense** – unless you are writing a report about something in the past.
14. You may include **photos**, **pictures**, **maps** and **diagrams** to present your information simply and clearly.

Conclusion

15. End with a concluding paragraph. It can be a **summary** of the report.
16. The information report writing frame will help you with this process.

INFORMATION REPORT WRITING FRAME

1. Decide
2. Plan it!
3. Draft it!
4. Check and change it!
5. Publish it!
6. Think about it!

Your name: _____
Date of writing: _____

Title

Choose a title that tells the reader what your report is about.

Introduction

Start the report with either:
- A statement that tells the audience what the text will be about
- A short description of the topic
- A definition of the topic

Body

- In the body of the report, give important facts about your topic.
- Organise the facts into paragraphs with headings.
- Your report can be about a person, an animal, an object or a place.

Person
Name
Age
Appearance (what they look like)
Personality
Occupation (their job)
History
Achievements (what makes this person unique or special)

Animal
Appearance
Habitat
Movement
Diet/food
Behaviour
Enemies
Life-cycle
Endangered species?

Object
Appearance
Parts
Functions
Features
Uses
Value

Place
Location
Climate
Geography
Population
Culture
History (historical buildings)
Interesting facts (what makes this place special or unique)

Pictures

Include pictures, photos, maps or diagrams if they help to present your information simply and clearly.

Conclusion

The final paragraph should sum up the report.

Checklist for information reports

Did you remember to do all of these things?
- Choose a **title** that informs the reader.
- Write an **introduction** that is either a **statement**, a **description** or a **definition**.
- Provide important information and facts in the **body of the report**.
- Organise the information into **paragraphs** with **headings**.
- Start each paragraph with a **topic sentence**.
- Include **pictures, photos**, **maps** or **diagrams** that could help the reader to understand the topic.
- Write a **concluding paragraph** to summarise the report.

Did you show the following writing skills?
- Use **formal** or **impersonal** language.
- Write a **glossary** for the reader if there is a lot of **technical language** in your report.
- **Vary** the sentences. (**Do not** start each sentence with the name of the topic.)
- Use the **present tense** (or **past tense** if it is a historical topic).
- Check **spelling** and **punctuation**.
- Write **neatly**.

EXPLANATION

Purpose of explanation
A good explanation should tell your reader about how something works or why something happens. You will need to be clear in your explanation. Before writing an explanation, you should gather as much information as possible on the topic.

Audience for explanation
Your audience is someone who wants to know how something works or why something happens.

Forms of explanation
Explanation writing has many forms, including:

> non-fiction books   manuals   science books   charts
> posters   study books   encyclopaedias   internet sites

Research for explanation
Before you write a piece of explanation writing, you must do a lot of **research**. Start by asking yourself questions about the topic. The questions you ask yourself will be the same questions that the reader will want to ask!
- How does it happen/work?
- Why does it happen/work?
- When does it happen/work?
- Where does it happen/work?
- What is the use of it?
- What else do I know?

WRITING: FICTION AND NON-FICTION

When you go to the dentist, you will find lots of information leaflets in the waiting room. Many of them explain the causes of tooth decay. These are examples of explanation writing!

Here is an example of *explanation writing*. It was written by Rebecca Mc Ginty on the topic of 'How Guide Dogs Are Trained'.

Explanation Writing

| Rebecca Mc Ginty Fifth Class | St Safan's NS, Castlefinn, Co. Donegal | 'How Guide Dogs Are Trained' |

Guide dogs are trained to help the blind and children with autism.

From six weeks old, puppies are looked after by volunteers that look after the breeding stock all year round. They trade breeding stock with lots of other countries: Germany, Korea and the United States of America.

During their first few weeks puppies are micro-chipped and given a vet exam. Then they start the basics of house training. After the house training stage, at about eight weeks, the puppies go to a Puppy-Walker.

irish guide dogs for the blind

A Puppy-Walker is a person who volunteers to foster the puppies for 12 to 15 months. This is another stage of the pups' training. During the first year Puppy-Walkers dedicate their time to training the pup. They teach the young dog how to be obedient and take them on daily walks to get used to the traffic and also all the human beings.

At one year old, the puppy leaves its Puppy-Walker and joins up to forty other dogs at the training centre in Cork. This part of the training can last for three to five months. Trainers now work in groups of five to six dogs daily, testing each dog's skill and intelligence, all while reinforcing a positive attitude.

Dogs are taken on walks to get used to the city bustle, the noise and the traffic. They are also taught to cross the roads, avoid obstacles and stop at kerbs. The dogs are taken to shopping centres, on buses, trains, lifts and so on. They are also taught to behave in restaurants.

If the now fully grown dog finishes early training and meets the high standards needed to become a fully trained guide dog, it will move on to another stage of training for three months. After that the dogs enter the last stage. They are perfected, so that he/she will find the perfect owner. The trainer will check if the dog walks slow or fast, if it prefers the city noise or the quiet country. From these traits, the pup is matched with the owner that would suit that dog. Getting the match right is crucial; a lot of effort goes into the matching up. Now the dog is ready to graduate as a fully trained guide dog. Then they go on a three-week course together at the training centre. After they have finished the course they return to the owner's home. The instructor visits the home weekly to help get the dog used to the new routes.

A guide dog will usually begin to tire at the age of ten and at this time the centre will begin to think of retiring the dog. This can be difficult for both dog and owner because they have spent many years together. The owner will often keep the dog as a pet for the remainder of their lives. If they choose not to, they find a nice home for these hard-working dogs. The owner is left with a new dog as soon as possible. It can be hard to adjust to life with a new dog that has a new personality, but soon they become the best of friends.

Here are my top tips for explanation writing.

Top tips for explanation
Research
1. **Choose a topic** that you are curious about and do a lot of research on it. As you research the topic, **take notes** on any key information that you will use in your explanation writing.

Explanation
2. Include a **question word** in the **title** of your explanation, e.g. how or why. Keep this question word in mind as you write your explanation, e.g. *How does a plane take off?*
3. Write a short introduction that provides a **description** or a **definition**.
4. The body of your explanation should be broken into clear sections that answer **how**, **why**, **when**, **where** and **what**.
5. State the **key facts** in **concise** sentences. Try to include **interesting facts** that will engage the reader.
6. Provide a **glossary** if there is a lot of **technical language** in your explanation.
7. Use the **present tense**.
8. Include **diagrams**, **charts** or **illustrations** if they will help to explain the topic.
9. Use a wide variety of time connectives.
10. End with a concluding paragraph. It could be a **summary**, **recommendation** or **general comment** about its use or history.

EXPLANATION WRITING FRAME

1. Decide
2. Plan it!
3. Draft it!
4. Check and change it!
5. Publish it!
6. Think about it!

Your name: _____

Date of writing: _____

Title
Choose a title that includes a question word, e.g. how or why.

Introduction
Provide a short description or definition.

Body
Explanation of how, why, when, where and what.

Something happens	Something works
• How does it happen?	• How does it work?
• Why does it happen?	• Why does it work?
• When does it happen?	• When does it work?
• Where does it happen?	• Where does it work?
• What is the use of it?	• What is the use of it?
• What else do I know?	• What else do I know?

Conclusion
Summary, recommendation or general comment.

Checklist for explanation

Did you remember to do all of these things?
- Choose a **title** that includes a **question word**.
- Write an introduction that contains a short **description** or **definition**.
- Provide important information and facts in the **body of the explanation**.
- Divide the body of your explanation into clear sections that answer **how**, **why**, **when**, **where** and **what**.
- Give a **complete** explanation.
- Provide a conclusion that contains a summary, recommendation or a general comment about its use or history.

Did you show the following writing skills?
- Use **formal** or **impersonal** language.
- Write a **glossary** for the reader if there is a lot of **technical language** in your explanation.
- Use **concise** sentences.
- Use the **present tense**.
- Check **spelling** and **punctuation**.
- Write **neatly**.

PERSUASION

The purpose of persuasion writing is to give your point of view and to **persuade** the reader (audience) to agree with you.

The important things are to be **positive** (not angry) and to make sure you are **right**! Think of all the reasons you can to support your opinion and argue against other views.

Purpose of persuasion
Persuasion writing can convince the reader to **buy** something or **support** something.

Audience
Before you write a persuasion text you must first think of your audience. Ask yourself **who** you are trying to convince. You must focus your argument on your audience, e.g. if your argument is that your school should have a longer lunch break, then your audience will be the teaching staff, principal and parents.

Forms of persuasion
Persuasion writing has many forms, including:

> debates   letters   emails   advertising
> newspaper articles   brochures   leaflets   essays
> speeches   book blurbs

Here is an example of persuasion writing. It was written by Aoibheann de Paor, who was writing to Kilkenny Borough Council to persuade them about the location of a new skate park.

Persuasion

| Aoibheann de Paor Sixth Class | Gaelscoil Osraí Cill Chainnigh | Letter to Kilkenny Borough Council: 'The new skate park in Kilkenny should be located…' |

Gaelscoil Osraí
Loch Buí
Cill Chainnigh
23 October 2013

Kilkenny Borough Council
Kilkenny

Dear Sir/Madam,

    I am writing this letter to persuade you, the hard-working members of Kilkenny Borough Council, to build the skate park on the Closh, on the Jail Road, opposite the Omniplex. In my opinion, it should be situated there based upon my following arguments.

    Firstly, I feel strongly that the skate park should be located on the Closh because it is the correct size for a skate park. It also has a beautiful and bright mural in its background, which was artistically painted by the talented Loreto Secondary School art students last year. It also has an existing boundary wall on each side, which makes the Closh an extremely safe place to skate as well as giving the financial benefit of not having to build a new wall.

    Furthermore, the Closh is very centrally located, in close proximity to a lot of the primary schools in the city, e.g. Presentation Primary School on Parnell Street, St John of God Primary School on Patrick's Street and CBS Primary School on Stephen's Street. These schools could use the skate park as part of their physical education schemes and encourage children from around the area to use the skate park. In this way, the skate park would not go to waste.

WRITING: FICTION AND NON-FICTION

In addition, I believe the Omniplex would support the skate park if it was built on the Closh. They would benefit from the increase of the local youth in the area because the people using the skate park would be drawn into the cinema to watch a film after skating.

I advise you to take my ideas on board, since I have thought them through thoroughly. I feel that the Closh is the best location for the skate park because of the support from the Omniplex and the local schools that would regularly use the skate park for various types of physical education. It will regenerate the site by changing it from a dreary, overgrown field to a wonderful facility for everyone to enjoy.

Thank you for reading my letter. I hope my arguments have persuaded you to build the skate park on the Closh. I look forward to hearing from you in the future.

Yours faithfully,

Aoibheann de Paor

Here are my top tips for persuasion writing.

Top tips for persuasion

1. Think about your **audience** before you begin to write.
2. At the **start** of your persuasion writing, **introduce your point of view** in a clear way, e.g. *School lunch breaks should be much longer.*
3. Include **three or more points** or reasons that support your point of view.
4. Write **one** point in each paragraph. Give **examples** that help to explain each point.

5. Think about the arguments that others may have **against** your point of view so that you can argue back, e.g. *Some people believe…but is this true?*
6. **Involve the reader** by asking them questions that encourage them to think, e.g. *Do you want?*
7. Be **positive** – make it seem obvious that everyone should agree with you. Use words such as of course, surely, no wonder, etc.
8. Use the **present** tense.
9. Your conclusion should repeat what you believe and the reasons for this. You could finish with a snappy slogan, e.g. *Longer breaks means happier children!*
10. The persuasion writing frame will help you with this process.

PERSUASION WRITING FRAME

1. Decide
2. Plan it!
3. Draft it!
4. Check and change it!
5. Publish it!
6. Think about it!

Your name: _____
Date of writing: _____

Title
Choose a title that explains the aim of the persuasion.

Point of view
Give your opinion on the topic.

Although not everyone would agree, I would like to argue that…
OR
I would like to persuade you that…

Series of points in order of importance
I have several reasons for arguing this point of view. My first reason is…

Furthermore…

I ask you this: do you want…?

Therefore, although some people might argue that… I believe that…

Conclusion
Repeat what you believe and the reasons for this. Finish with a snappy slogan (optional).

Checklist for persuasion

Did you remember to do all of these things?
- Introduce your point of view at the **start**.
- Give **three or more reasons** that support your view.
- Start a **new paragraph** for each new point.
- Give **examples** that explain your point of view.
- Think about the arguments that others might have against your point of view – and **argue back**.
- **Involve the reader** by asking them questions.
- **Conclude** by repeating what you believe and the reasons for this.

Did you show the following writing skills?
- Use **persuasive** language. Make it seem obvious that the reader should agree with you by using **positive** words: of course, surely, no wonder, etc.
- Ask **direct questions** of the reader so that they are involved, e.g. *Don't you agree that…?*
- Use **connectives**: however, on the other hand, despite this, etc.
- Use the **present** tense.
- Write a conclusion reinforcing your point of view; perhaps finish with a snappy **slogan**.
- Check **spelling** and **punctuation**.
- Write **neatly**.

WRITING: FICTION AND NON-FICTION

Once your class has learned how to write persuasion texts, try challenging another class to a debate!

Leaflets and posters

Leaflets and posters involve persuasion writing. The purpose of a leaflet or poster is to convince the reader to buy a product, use a service or attend an event.

Here are my top tips for leaflets and posters.

Top tips for leaflets and posters
1. The leaflet or poster must be easy to read, so **don't use** too many words.
2. Choose words that will **grab the reader's attention**, e.g. alliteration.
3. **Hook the reader** by asking a question or making a joke.
4. Use **persuasive** language or **slogans** to convince the reader, e.g. *Don't delay – visit today!*
5. If you are advertising something, explain **why** it is so good. Use exciting adjectives and superlatives.
6. Appeal to your reader's **senses**: sight, hearing, touch, taste and smell.
7. The **design** should be attractive and eye-catching. Use **photos** or images that will interest the reader.
8. Choose the most important point and give that the most **space**.

9. Think about where your leaflet or poster will be displayed. This will help you to decide on a **size**.
10. The leaflet/poster writing frame will help you with this process.

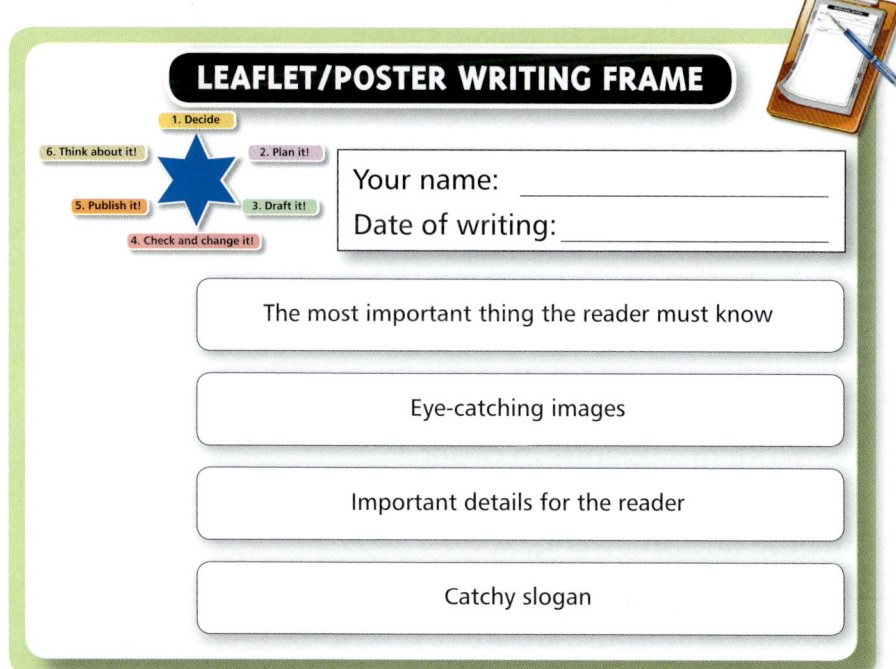

LEAFLET/POSTER WRITING FRAME

1. Decide
2. Plan it!
3. Draft it!
4. Check and change it!
5. Publish it!
6. Think about it!

Your name: _____
Date of writing: _____

The most important thing the reader must know

Eye-catching images

Important details for the reader

Catchy slogan

Checklist for leaflets and posters

Did you remember to do all of these things?
- **Grab the reader's attention**.
- Give the most **space** to the most important point.
- Explain **why** the product or service is so good.
- Appeal to the reader's **senses**.
- Create an attractive, eye-catching **design**.
- Use **photos** or images.
- Choose the right **size** for your poster or leaflet.

WRITING: FICTION AND NON-FICTION

Did you show the following writing skills?
- Use **few words** so that the message is clear.
- Use **persuasive** language, **alliteration** or **slogans**.
- Use **exciting** adjectives and superlatives.
- Ask a **question** or make a **joke**.
- Check **spelling** and **punctuation**.
- Write **neatly**.

DISCUSSION

Purpose of discussion
We write discussions in order to present different points of view on something. A discussion text will show the evidence and information from both sides. Before writing your discussion, you should gather as much information as possible on the topic.

Audience for discussion
Your audience is someone who wants to know all about something and wants to understand the different points of view. This person will want to make up their own mind once they have all the information.

Forms of discussion
Discussion writing has many forms, including:

> debates leaflets posters letters to the editor
> newspaper articles essays

Research for discussion
Before you write a piece of discussion writing, you must do a lot of **research**. You will have many **sources of information** available to you:
- Books
- Newspapers and magazines
- Internet
- Knowledge you already have
- Knowledge your friends already have

Use these sources to gather lots of information. Then divide all the information into key points, providing evidence to back up each of the points.

Once you have done all of this research, you will be ready to write your discussion!

> Here is an example of *discussion writing*. It was written by Aimee Cronin, who was discussing this topic: 'Are zoos good or bad for animals?'

WRITING: FICTION AND NON-FICTION

Discussion

Aimee Cronin
Sixth Class

Scoil Aiseirí
Chríost NS
Cork City

'Are zoos good or bad for animals?'

In this discussion, I am going to present to you the many reasons why zoos are good or bad for animals. Firstly, here are the reasons why I think zoos are good for animals.

Zoos protect animals. They save the animals from being hunted by poachers. Poachers are people who illegally hunt and kill animals to sell them for money. For example, the crocodile is widely hunted for its valuable hide and skin, which is used to make handbags and shoes. Zoos also protect animals in danger of extinction. Some examples of these are hippos, pandas, snow leopards and crocodiles. The Siamese crocodile is now extinct in the wild. You can only see them on crocodile farms. Elephants are mainly hunted for their ivory tusks, but poachers sometimes hollow out the elephants' legs to be used as a rubbish bin. The rhino is the most endangered species in the world. They are hunted mainly for their ivory horns. Africans believe that a rhino horn can cure anything. This is why I agree that zoos protect endangered animals.

Some people think that zoos are good because they protect animals from each other. Zoos are a safe environment for animals. Most animals such as the lions, tigers and hyenas are carnivores. This means that they eat meat and attack other animals. These animals are called predators. The animals they hunt are called prey animals. In zoos, prey animals are protected from other predators.

Zoos are good for the animals because they treat sick animals. They also have a vet who can give the animals annual check-ups and treat them. If an animal becomes ill in the zoo, it can be treated straight away, but in the wild the animal can spread diseases to others. In the wild, when an animal becomes ill or injured, it is left to die and will be easy prey for predators. This means the animal is more likely to die. However, in a zoo the animal would be treated straight away and is more likely to survive. This is another reason why zoos are good for animals.

Zoos are beneficial to animals because they can breed in a safe environment. In the wild, the pregnant mother has a chance of getting injured and losing her offspring. In the zoo, the pregnant mother can be monitored so that the offspring will have a better chance of surviving. In the wild, the offspring are easy prey and will most likely be killed. This, of course, wouldn't happen in a zoo. This also makes it easier on the mother.

Zoos are good for animals because they get properly taken care of. They get the correct food and the right amount of it. They have a shelter and also zoos try to replicate the natural habitat of the animal so that it feels more comfortable and gets used to its surroundings. Water is always available to the animals instead of them searching for hours in the wild.

In order to give a balanced view, I shall now give you the reasons why zoos are bad for the animals.

It is known that zoos are bad for the animals because they take away their freedom. Animals were meant to be wild and not caged in. In zoos, animals can't roam around or discover. They are trapped in the same area every day. This makes them lose their natural instincts, such as foraging, hunting and creating their own habitat. Animals in zoos don't know how to find their own food, since the zookeepers do this for them. This is one of the main reasons zoos are bad for animals.

Zoos are not good for animals because most of the animals are not native to the country. The zoo tries to replicate the animal's habitat but it will never be correct. The climate is also incorrect. Penguins and polar bears are often in warmer habitats than they should be. Gorillas, lions, tigers and crocodiles are in colder habitats than they should be. This is a major reason why zoos are bad for animals.

Zoos are terrible for animals because some animals are separated from their families and sent to other zoos using breeding programmes. The animals may get lonely. The animals are also constantly on display and getting disturbed by humans. They may get annoyed and angry. A life in a zoo cannot be very fun!

The problem is that many zoos are too poor to look after the animals properly. Some are unclean and unhealthy for the animal. This can make the animal become very ill. Some zoos can be very cruel to animals and don't treat them well. This shortens the lifespan of the animal – and the animal lives out its life terrified of humans.

These are the different reasons why zoos are good and bad. It's now up to you to decide on your opinion. My opinion is that even though animals should be left free, they are well taken care of in zoos.

Top tips for discussion

Research

1. Use many different sources to **research** the topic. As you research the topic, **take notes** on any **key points** and gather evidence to support each key point.

Discussion

2. Ask a **question** in the title, e.g. *Should children wear school uniforms to school?*
3. Give a **brief overview** of the issue and the different points of view.
4. Give three or four reasons **FOR** and three or four reasons **AGAINST**.
5. Do not become personally involved in the argument. Instead of saying *I think*, say *many people believe* or *it is known that* or *some people say*… You must present both sides fairly, not just say what you think, until the conclusion.
6. Use a **separate paragraph** for each key point.
7. Use **connectives**: however, on the other hand, although, despite, etc.
8. Use the **present** tense.
9. Conclude with a **summary** or **recommendation**. Give your own opinion in the conclusion; however, you must explain your reasons for it.
10. The discussion writing frame will help you with this process.

DISCUSSION WRITING FRAME

1. Decide
2. Plan it!
3. Draft it!
4. Check and change it!
5. Publish it!
6. Think about it!

Your name: _____
Date of writing: _____

Title
Ask a question in the title.

Issue
Give a brief explanation of the issue and the different points of view.

Arguments for
The people who agree with this idea (such as…) say that…

They also argue that…

Another point they make is that…

Arguments against
However, there are also strong arguments against this point of view…

They also argue that…

Another point they make is that…

Conclusion
Give a summary or recommendation.
Finish with your own opinion – and your reasons for it.

WRITING: FICTION AND NON-FICTION

Checklist for discussion

Did you remember to do all of these things?
- **Ask a question** in the title.
- Give a **brief explanation** of the issue and the **different points of view**.
- Write three or four arguments **FOR**.
- Write three or four arguments **AGAINST**.
- Use a **separate paragraph** for each key point.
- Give **reasons** for each point of view.
- Conclude with a **summary** or **recommendation**.

Did you show the following writing skills?
- Use **connectives**: however, on the other hand, despite this, etc.
- Use the **present** tense.
- Check **spelling** and **punctuation**.
- Write **neatly**.

RESPONSE

The purpose of response writing is to describe personal reactions to a subject or event. Response writing may be used for feedback, an assessment, or a review.

Reviews are helpful because they give the reader information about something they are interested in, e.g. a book, play or film. When you write a review, give your reader information along with your own opinion. Look for some examples of reviews in your favourite magazine, newspaper or website so you can see how they are written.

Purpose of response
Responses are written as a personal reaction to a subject or event. Responses might be about live performances, art shows, community events, TV shows, restaurants, movies, computer games, websites, books or music.

Purpose of reviews
The purpose of a review is so that the reader can find out more about something they are interested in. A review will give information of the item being reviewed and also provide the reviewer's personal opinion, i.e. whether they think something is good or bad – and why. Sometimes a review gives a star rating from one to five.

Audience for reviews
Your audience is someone interested in finding out what a particular book, film, music, play or restaurant is like.

Forms of response
Response writing has many forms, including:

> book review   film review   event review
> restaurant review   personal response

WRITING: FICTION AND NON-FICTION

> Here is an example of response writing. It was written by Aisling Kenny, who was reviewing a book called *Over the Wall* by Renate Ahrens.

Response

| Aisling Kenny | Scoil Bhríde NS | Book review |
| Sixth Class | Co. Galway | *Over the Wall* by Renate Ahrens |

Title: *Over the Wall*
Author: Renate Ahrens

The book I am reviewing is called *Over the Wall*. It is a children's fiction book with a historical setting. The story is set in Hamburg, Germany, after the fall of the Berlin Wall. It tells of the life of a girl called Karo and the impact of the Berlin Wall on her life.

Karo lives in West Germany with her mother in the early 1990s. Recently, the Berlin Wall has been knocked over, reuniting West and East Germany. Karo's mother always told her that her father had died in a car accident when she was younger. One day a strange man comes to the door of their house. Karo's mother seems to know this man from her past. She starts to spend more and more time with this man but Karo does not approve of this and is jealous. Karo starts acting out: she cuts her hair and starts to skip school. She leaves home and goes to live with her grandfather. Karo and her friend find out that the man is a movie writer. They decide to go and watch a film he has written. As Karo is watching the film, she realises that it is based on the story of her mother and father and how they were separated by the Berlin Wall. By the end of the story, Karo has confronted the strange man and has realised that he is actually her father. Although he has since remarried and has a son, he is now divorced. The book finishes with Karo, her mother and her father moving to Berlin to start a new life together.

My favourite character is Karo. I like this character because she is very stubborn and independent. She's able to stand up for herself and fights for what she believes in. I think this is a good trait to have. My favourite part of the story was when Karo and her friend went to watch the film. I liked this because it shows the pieces of Karo's life fitting back together like a jigsaw.

Overall, I really liked this book. There was nothing I disliked about the way this book was written. Personally, I would recommend this book for girls aged 10 to 12. It was a brilliant story.

Rating: 10/10

Here are my top tips for response writing.

Top tips for response

1. **Take notes** on the item to be reviewed. Do this while you are reading the book, watching the film, etc. This will help you to remember all the points you want to make in your review.
2. Give **factual details** of the item, e.g. the title of the book or film, the name of the author or director, etc. Identify the **genre**.
3. Give a **description** of the main characters, setting and plot – without giving away any surprises!
4. Use lots of **descriptive adjectives**: interesting, boring, adventurous, exciting, confusing, thrilling, etc.
5. If the item is a play or a film, comment on the **setting**, **scenery**, **costume**, **actors** and **lighting**.
6. If the item is a book, comment on the **writing style**.
7. Give your **personal opinion** of the item. Say what you liked and didn't like – and **why**.
8. Give a **recommendation** for the kind of reader who might enjoy the item. Include a **star rating**, if you like.
9. Remember that your review should be informative and entertaining.
10. The response writing frame will help you with this process.

RESPONSE WRITING FRAME

1. Decide
2. Plan it!
3. Draft it!
4. Check and change it!
5. Publish it!
6. Think about it!

Your name: _____
Date of writing: _____

Title
Name the item being reviewed.

Introduction
Give a brief description of the item and its genre.

Body
Describe the elements of the item: characters, setting, plot, etc.

Give your personal opinion of the item. State what you liked and didn't like – and why.

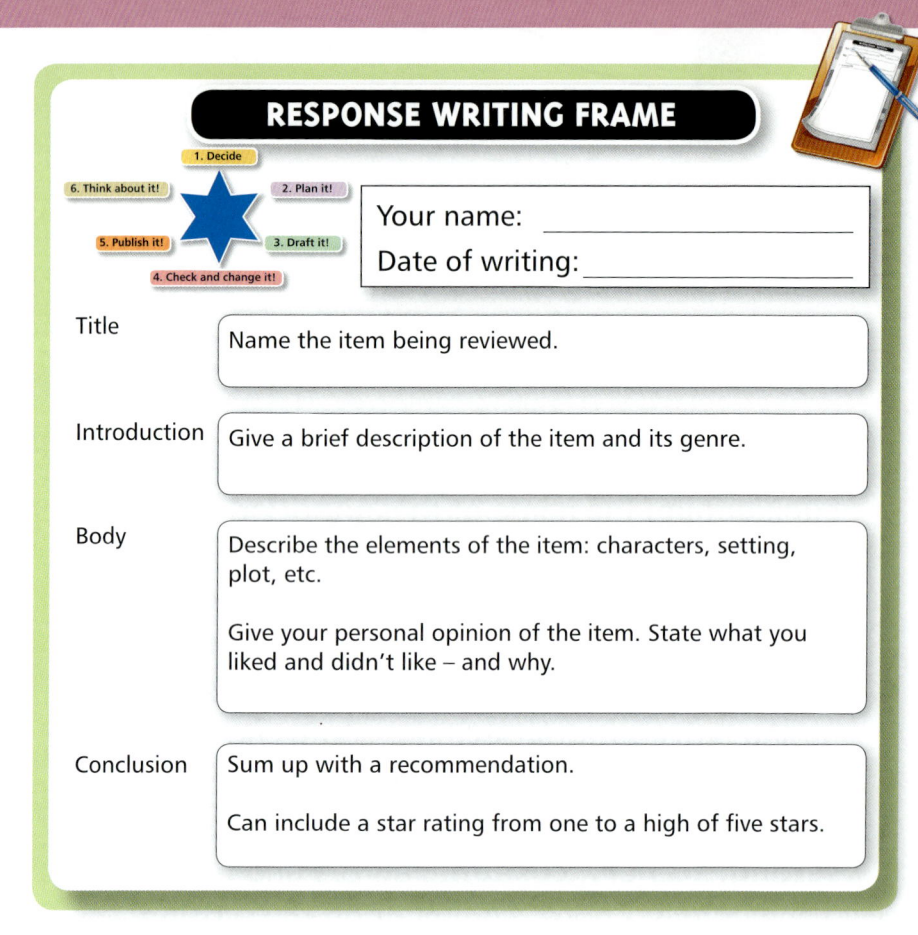

Conclusion
Sum up with a recommendation.

Can include a star rating from one to a high of five stars.

Checklist for response

Did you remember to do all of these things?
- Give **factual details** of the item being reviewed.
- Identify the **genre**.
- **Describe** the item, e.g. main characters, setting and plot.
- If the item is a play or film, comment on the setting, scenery, costume, actors, lighting, etc.

- If the item is a book, comment on the **writing style**.
- Write a **personal response**. Say what you liked and didn't like – and why.
- Give a **recommendation** and a star rating if you like.

Did you show the following writing skills?
- Write in an **informative and entertaining** way.
- Use **descriptive** adjectives.
- Check **spelling** and **punctuation**.
- Write **neatly**.

NARRATIVE

A narrative is a story or an account of events and experiences. Narratives can be true or fictitious (made up). Writing a narrative is a bit like following a recipe.

Purpose of narratives

A narrative can tell a story, provide entertainment, make an audience think about an issue, teach the reader a lesson or make them feel excited.

There are many different **types** of narratives, including:

| stories | poems | ballads | folk tales | fairy tales |
| plays | legends | myths | fables | |

Narrative forms

Narrative writing comes in many forms, including:

> picture books   storybooks   short story collections
> film scripts   novels   comics   graphic novels
> poetry anthologies

> Writing stories is cool! It's your chance to let your imagination run free and to impress everyone with your amazing writing talent. Before we start, let's look at some words that you need to know:
> - *Fiction*: writing that has been made up
> - *Non-fiction*: writing that is based on fact
> - *Plot*: the order of events in a story; the events link together and lead to the end of the story
> - *Setting*: the place and time of the story
> - *Characters*: the people in the story

How to write a narrative

There is a recipe that you can follow if you want to write a narrative. The first part of the recipe involves **brainstorming**. Brainstorming means using your mind and imagination to think of lots of ideas. Write down all the ideas you have about the topic or story.

Like all recipes, you will need **ingredients**. Usually, narratives have four main parts or ingredients. The four ingredients all begin with the letter P:
- **P**lace and time
- **P**eople
- **P**roblem
- **P**roblem solved

Think of any story you know and you will be able to identify the four ingredients that make up a narrative. Let's take *Little Red Riding Hood* as an example.

- The story opens with a description of the **place and time**…
  The setting is the place and time of your story. You want to make your readers feel like they are inside that setting. Use your **senses** to go into the setting yourself and give as many descriptive details as you can. Describe clearly what you see, hear, touch, taste and smell.

  > Long, long ago in a little village at the edge of a deep forest, there lived a little girl and her mother and father.

- The **people** or **characters** are introduced…
  The next ingredient is the people or characters. Creating characters is like meeting new people. To get to know your characters, think of clever questions to ask them. Then make up the answers your characters would give!

> This little girl was the sweetest, kindest child there ever was. She was always dressed in a pretty red cloak and hood that her mother had made for her. It was because of this cloak that everyone began calling her Little Red Riding Hood.

- **The problem…**

  Ingredient number three is **conflict**. Conflict involves all the problems or complications in a story. Problems are a very important ingredient. They keep your reader interested and they encourage the reader to keep reading. The reader wants to find out how the problems are solved.

  When writing narratives, you need a problem for your character(s) and this problem needs to be solved. Remember not to solve all the problems too early in your story – because you want to keep your reader guessing as to what is going to happen!

  Don't forget that the problems in the story will affect your character's feelings or **emotions**. A character who has a big problem might feel angry at first. You can make the character show this emotion by having them stomping around. Or if your character feels worried, you can show this by having them bite their nails.

  When the problem is fixed, your character's feelings will change. Now your character might feel proud or happy.

> Little Red Riding Hood's mother asked her to take some food to her ill grandmother who lived on the other side of the forest. Her mother warned Little Red Riding Hood not to talk to strangers. However, Little Red Riding Hood forgot her mother's instructions and when she met Mr Wolf, she told him where she was going. Mr Wolf rushed off, tricked the grandmother by pretending to be Little Red Riding Hood and swallowed the grandmother whole! Then he dressed up as the grandmother and Little Red Riding Hood came knocking on the door…

WRITING: FICTION AND NON-FICTION

- The **problem is solved**…
  The final ingredient in the recipe is when the problem is solved. This is the **ending**. How the story ends is very important. You want your readers to feel it was worth their while reading the story to the end. If you write an interesting ending, your readers will be satisfied.

  Your character needs to **fix the problems** that remain. That is why the reader kept reading! Now is your chance to write the big moment of the story. It is called the **resolution**. The resolution comes when all the problems are finally solved or fixed.

> When poor Little Red Riding Hood arrived, Mr Wolf swallowed her whole too! The problem was finally solved when the woodcutter arrived at the cottage. The woodcutter realised what the wolf had done and then saved the day by rescuing Little Red Riding Hood and her grandmother from the nasty wolf's belly.

Little Red Riding Hood is a very simple example, but it clearly shows the four main parts or ingredients of a narrative.

After you have written the narrative, you might want to think again about the **title**. Remember to pick a title that will grab your readers' attention.

Sharing your story

Now that the cooking is over, it is time to share the finished product! There are many different ways to share your story. Here are just a few ideas:

- Read your story out loud
- Make a recording of your story and add some sound effects
- Turn your story into a book and create a suitable cover
- Go on the internet and post your story on an online story site (ask an adult for permission and help with this)

How to write different genres of narrative
How to write horror stories
A good horror story should make your reader jump out of their seat with fright. You must have a **spooky setting**, e.g. an old mansion or a run-down fairground. Have a ghost, goblin, vampire or an unusual monster as the main character. Build up lots of **suspense** with describing words and short sentences. End with a surprise.

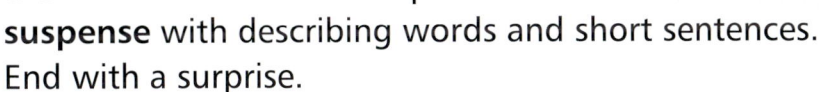

How to write adventure stories
A good adventure story should be very **exciting**. The characters are usually on a **journey** where lots of things happen to them along the way. Most adventure stories have happy endings.

The problem in the story must force the characters to go on a journey. Make the journey a dangerous one for the characters with lots of problems for them to overcome. Build up lots of **suspense** and **excitement** through a series of adventures, each one worse than the last.

How to write fantasy adventures
Fantasy adventure stories are adventure stories set in a **made-up world**. They usually include weird creatures like fairies and very nasty baddies.

Base your story on a **quest** (a journey to find something or someone). The setting is usually a made-up place. Have unusual characters who are not all human. Have lots of problems for the main character to overcome.

How to write mystery stories

Good mystery stories don't tell you immediately what's going on. You have to **figure it out** or wait until the end to find out.

Start with something **dramatic** or exciting to set the scene. Give the reader some clues as to what has happened; this will build up the **suspense**. Make the reader think they know what is going on. Have **mysterious** sounds, smells and lights to create suspense. Give the story away **a little bit at a time**. Try putting a **twist** at the end – to surprise the reader. Make sure everything is explained by the **end** of the story.

How to write historical stories

A historical story is always set in the **past**. The characters and objects in your story must match the time that the story is set in. You can't have the Vikings watching TV!

Historical stories are just adventure stories based on fact. Use **facts** from history to make the story sound realistic.

Make the characters talk and act like people did at that time in history.

Science fiction stories

A science fiction story is an adventure story in a **futuristic world**, maybe in space or on a different planet. Usually, science fiction stories involve a quest and lots of fancy gadgets.

Set the story in space or in the future. Usually the characters go on an adventure. There could be strange settings, hi-tech gadgets and machines – and even creatures from a different planet!

Humorous stories

A humorous story should make your readers **laugh**. Include funny characters. Include one dull character to make the funny characters seem even funnier. Turn everyday situations into funny, odd situations. Use **conversations** to make the reader laugh.

Myths and legends

Many of the oldest stories are called **myths** or **legends**. Nobody knows if these stories are true. Myths and legends tell stories of heroes and warriors, fantastic beasts and battles, magic and mystery. These stories were first passed on by word of mouth and later written down. In Ireland we have a wonderful collection of myths and legends. 'The Children of Lir' is a very famous Irish legend.

Fairy tales

Fairy tales are stories written specially for children, often about magical characters such as fairies, elves, goblins and giants. Sometimes the characters are animals. Hans Christian Andersen is famous for writing fairy tales. Examples of his stories include 'The Little Mermaid' and 'Thumbelina'.

> Sometimes I find it really difficult to think of good ideas for a story. When I need help to come up with a great plot, setting and characters, I draw pictures that show my story – just like a comic strip. Now I am ready to plan my story using these pictures. Now that I know in my head what is going to happen, I can write my first draft on the narrative writing frame (see p.176).

Using pictures to plan a story

You can use **pictures** along with the **four Ps** to help you plan your story. Draw a table like the one on the next page. List the four Ps and draw a picture for each one. Then examine each picture and write down what you see. This will help your imagination to come up with the details you need for your story.

The four Ps	Draw a picture of what you imagine	Examine your pictures and write down the details you notice
Place and time ● Where is the story set? ● When is the story set? ● How does the setting affect your senses?		
People/characters ● Who is involved in your story?		
Problem ● What is the problem or complication?		
Problem solved ● How is the problem solved? ● Is it a happy ending or not?		

WRITING: FICTION AND NON-FICTION

> If you find it difficult to draw your own pictures for the four Ps, try using pictures that are already available in books, magazines or comics. Find a picture that interests you. Then imagine yourself in that picture! Create a story based in that setting by following the recipe for the four Ps.

> Look out for the four Ps in this example of a narrative, entitled 'Home'.

HOME

David stomped angrily around the farm on which he lived with his bitter father and selfish brother. The farm was an isolated place made up of huge, lonely green fields and massive grey sheds. As far as the eye could see there were no houses or people. Except, in the far corner of the land, when David climbed the solitary oak tree he could just about see the hazy outline of the city. High up in the oak tree David somehow did not feel by himself, but rather felt connected to the enormous city beyond...

'Get down from that tree!' roared David's angry father, who was working with his selfish accomplice in the next field.

'You're not a child anymore,' his brother mocked.

David had learned not to argue with this duo, since they had the power to make his life even more hellish – especially now that his mother had left. David's father was like the branches near the top of the oak tree: thin, weak and twisted. His brother Patrick was like the branches closer to the bottom: broad and strong.

David knew there was only one thing he could do: escape! But how? He was only thirteen, he had no money and he was miles from the one person he could rely on...

Stories generally start with a description of where the story takes place: the **setting**.

Then the writer introduces the **characters**. Usually, no more than three characters are needed.

Start a new paragraph for each new event.

New paragraphs are also needed each time you introduce a change of time and place. A **connective** can be used at the start of a paragraph to show the reader how the story has moved on.

Here comes the problem. The rest of the plot will follow on from this event until the story reaches a good ending.

As dawn began to break, David, completely exhausted but still determined, set about finding his mother in the enormous city. He held the scrap of paper with his mother's address on it in front of him. And, for the first time, he wasn't worrying about being caught.

Now, by nightfall, his horrific journey was coming to an end. With tears of triumph streaming from his eyes, he slowly walked up to the large red door of his mother's new home. He knocked at the door and waited – then, when it opened, yellow light poured over him. He ran into his mother's arms. David was home at last.

> You can use connectives at the start of paragraphs to tell the reader about movements in time: after a while, suddenly, the next day, later, eventually, etc.
>
> Connectives can also be used to show a change of place: back at school, far away, on the other side of, etc.

The problem is **solved.**

> Here is an example of a *narrative*. It was written by Hannah Purcell and it is entitled 'My Kitten'.

Narrative

| Hannah Purcell Sixth Class | St Mochulla's NS Co. Clare | 'My Kitten' |

I watched the bundle of fur and hoped that it would not fall from my lap. My new kitten was an undernourished, neglected creature. I stroked her matted black and white fur as she began to purr. She wasn't particularly pretty or cute but I just couldn't help beginning to love her. The six-week-old kitten squeaked helplessly as we drove along the bumpy road. It seemed that every time she took a breath it was a huge effort for her.

'My kitten Squeak – isn't she so cute?' I said to my father.

'I suppose,' he replied thoughtfully. He glanced doubtfully at the kitten through the driver's mirror. He was sure she was too small and weak to ever survive or to be a useful farm cat, able to avoid moving machinery or keep rats away from the bags of meal and mice from the yard. She looked up at me with her huge trusting eyes, as if she knew that I was the one who would determine her future.

In the beginning, I would give her some milk in her little bowl. She would step into it and patter her delicate paws in it. Then she would scamper off, leaving a trail of milk paw prints behind her and little drops of milk would fall off her now glistening coat. Squeak seemed amazed at the farm; I suppose it must have seemed like a gigantic playground to her. With the tall spruce trees to climb, crumbling sheds to explore and tractors to investigate, she never grew bored. Sometimes she would walk across the lawn snatching at any flyaway leaves that crossed her path. She would often play in the hay bales, snapping and scratching at all the loose bits of straw as if they were alive. Squeak would chase any piece of string that I dangled in front of her. She loved to play with her tiny stuffed animal on the lawn. She used to poke it with her paw; it would roll away and she'd chase it again and again, getting very excited and pretending it was a mouse. The hens were an entertaining past-time for Squeak and she would spend hours gazing curiously in awe at them. Whenever we collected the eggs from the hens she would stand there waiting for a chance to sneak into their coop and pounce on these odd flapping creatures. If a hen escaped from the coop and ran around the yard, Squeak would always chase the over-excited hen. It was a strange sight watching a clumsy stick-legged hen, wobbling, squawking and bobbing around the yard. The hen would be no match for my nimble, mouse-catching, chicken-chasing, top-class kitten.

But it didn't last. After some time, my lovely kitten gradually grew weaker and wasn't running, chasing or playing anymore. For days she would just walk slowly around the farm with her head held low and a melancholy look on her face. When she squeaked it sounded more like a desperate cry for help rather than the comical way it used to sound. Now she didn't scamper over to me; she just slightly raised her head and kept walking.

The day before my birthday the river was flooded and the rain pelted down on the leaky, rusty, galvanised roof of Squeak's shed. I ran outside to the shed to give Squeak her supper. I nudged the little bowl towards her. She looked at it longingly but stayed shivering in her basket. I picked her up and carefully placed her down beside her bowl, but her now thin legs were trembling, struggling to stand. I scooped her up and held her close. Instead of clinging to my coat like she normally did she lay there limply. I had to hold her tight so that she wouldn't fall out of my arms. My father ran outside to see what was taking me so long. Then he saw Squeak.

'There's nothing more we can do now, Hannah: kittens don't always survive,' he told me.

Squeak seemed to gaze up at me with a pleading look in her eyes. I tried to convince Dad that we had to try. I knew he was remembering the time when I was eight and Puss's tiny paw got stuck in the fan belt of our car's engine and how stubborn I was when we argued over bringing Puss to the vet and how I didn't keep quiet until he agreed with me.

'All right,' was all he managed to say.

We put Squeak in a basket lined with blankets and carried it in beside the stove. We got two small bowls and filled one with water and the other with cat food. I kneeled down beside Squeak, waiting for her to either grow weaker or stronger. I stroked her gently and tried to listen to her breathing as she drifted in and out of sleep. I hoped her cold body was gradually becoming warmer. The only sounds were Squeak's raspy breathing and the fire crackling. Time passed so slowly and the clock seemed to freeze. I knelt there after everyone had gone to bed, staring into the fire and waiting for Squeak to wake up. When she finally woke, she struggled to get to her feet and wobbled slowly towards the food and water. She ate slowly – only eating a little. It was a miracle! Tears of joy came to my eyes. 'Squeak might just make it,' I thought to myself. I watched happily for a few minutes. But deep down I knew she was still weak and it would take a lot more than a few mouthfuls of food to revive her. Squeak wobbled slowly to her feet and lay down beside the comforting fire and drifted into a deep sleep. 'All I can do now is wait until the morning and see if she improves,' I said to myself. I was still worried that Squeak wouldn't survive the night but I eventually fell asleep.

In the morning I woke when someone rapped loudly on the door. I headed downstairs but my mother was already there. It was only the postman delivering a parcel. Just then, Mum made a shriek of terror. Something alive, well and moving brushed against her heels and then scampered off. It was the best birthday present I could ever hope for.

Here are my top tips for narrative writing.

Top tips for narrative

1. **Plan** your story before you write it and remember the **four Ps**: place, people, problem and problem solved.
2. The **beginning** of your story is very important. You don't want your reader nodding off, so you need to grab the reader's attention from the very beginning! Start with something exciting.
3. Use interesting adjectives and adverbs to **describe** settings, characters, events and moods. Describe everything so that the reader can see, feel, taste and hear what is happening in the story. Describe the things in your story by comparing them to other things (**simile**), e.g. *He **looked like** Frankenstein's monster*. Use sound (**onomatopoeia**), e.g. *The stairs **creaked** with every step I took*. Use **metaphors**, e.g. *The frosty air chased people and bit at their fingers and toes as they left their homes in the morning.*
4. As you write your story, use **paragraphs** to make the order of events clear to your reader.
5. Avoid using common words, e.g. nice. Use more dramatic words: brilliant, amazing, etc. A **thesaurus** will help you with this.

6. Keep your story clear: **don't lose the reader.** Stick to your plan. Always read back over your story while you are writing and also when it is finished. If any part of your story seems unclear, then you need to change it. Remember, if it is unclear to you, then the reader will be completely confused! Your response partner should help you with this during the writing process.
7. Let the characters talk (**dialogue**) so the reader knows what kind of people they are. However, do **not** overuse dialogue.
8. Decide from the start who the **narrator** will be. The narrator is the person telling the story – either a character in the story or someone watching the events. In other words, you are either in the story or you are not. Don't get mixed up!
9. The **ending** must be interesting. The last line is particularly important. The ending must **resolve** the problem that happened in the middle of the story. Remember: it doesn't always have to be a happy ending.
10. The narrative writing frame will help you with this process.

NARRATIVE WRITING FRAME

1. Decide
2. Plan it!
3. Draft it!
4. Check and change it!
5. Publish it!
6. Think about it!

Your name: _____

Date of writing: _____

Title

Choose an interesting title.

Place and time

Use all of your senses to describe the setting.

Set the tone and mood.

The reader needs to know all of these things about the setting:
- Where is it?
- What does it look like?
- Who lives there?
- What do they do there?
- What is it like to be there?
- How do you get there?
- What year, month and date is it?
- When does the story take place (past, present or future)?

People or characters

The reader needs to know all of these things about the characters:
- What do they look like?
- What age are they?
- What do they like or dislike?
- What kind of personality do they have?

Problem

There can be one or more problems that cause conflict for the characters.

This problem affects the characters' normal lives and makes different things happen.

The excitement and suspense build around the problem.

Try not to solve the problem too quickly; think of other problems that could arise.

Problem solved

The problem is resolved in the ending.

Checklist for narrative

Did you remember to do all of these things?
- Plan your story before beginning to write.
- Pay attention to the four Ps.
- Choose an exciting **title**.
- Write an exciting **beginning** to the story.
- Describe the setting, characters and events by using your **senses**.
- Organise your story into **paragraphs**.
- Keep your story **clear** so that the reader can follow it; choose a clear **narrator**.
- Resolve the problem with a satisfying **ending**.

Did you show the following writing skills?
- Use interesting **adjectives** and **adverbs**.
- Use **simile**, **metaphor**, **onomatopoeia** and dramatic vocabulary.
- Write interesting **dialogue** that tells us something about the characters.
- Create **suspense**.
- Use the **first person** or **third person** narrative.
- Check **spelling** and **punctuation**.
- Write **neatly**.

How to plan a character

Characters are the people, animals or creatures that the story is about. In fact, characters can even be aliens, ghosts or monsters! The characters act out the story like actors on a stage. The most important one is called the **main character**. When writing narratives, your characters must be interesting so that the reader will care about them and want to read more.

Before writing your story, you need to take some time to think about your characters. You need to be clear in your mind about what your characters look like; how they dress; what they would say or do in different situations (their personalities); how they feel inside; and what other characters think of them.

When you are planning your characters, you must always keep in mind the four Ps – and think about how your character will fit into the recipe!

Using pictures to plan a character

You can also use pictures to plan your characters. Have a look at these images of characters.

Now try answering the following questions for each of the characters:
- What is the character's name?
- What age are they?
- What makes them a hero/heroine?
- What makes them a villain?
- What do they look like?
- Where do they come from?
- What are their special talents or powers?
- What are they like?
- What is their personality?
- What are their plans?
- What way do they speak?

Use your imagination to help you find answers to all of these questions. Imagine that you are interviewing the character and that you are asking them these questions directly. Record all the answers and use them in your narrative.

CHARACTER PROFILE WRITING FRAME

1. Decide
2. Plan it!
3. Draft it!
4. Check and change it!
5. Publish it!
6. Think about it!

Your name: _____
Date of writing: _____

- Human with long black hair and pointed ears
- Alien wearing a strange helmet
- Lady with long black fingernails
- Teenager running as fast as the wind

- angry
- upset
- excited
- proud
- annoyed
- cheated
- afraid
- jealous
- brave
- bored
- kind

- run away
- steal
- fight
- rescue
- help
- tell
- explore

- trust
- distrust
- admire
- like
- dislike
- believe

	CHARACTER 1	CHARACTER 2	CHARACTER 3
Draw the character: appearance and clothing			
Write the character's name or nickname			
Write some words to describe the character's personality or behaviour			
Write about what will happen to the character at different points in your story			
What do other characters think of this character?			

180

Keep this poem in mind when you are writing narratives.

Recipe for a Story
by Michaela Morgan

Take an introduction.
Blend in atmosphere.
Stir in description and conversation.
Spice it up with suspense, humour or adventure.
Allow to rise.
Cook thoroughly, checking it from time to time.
Add the finishing touch – a good final sentence.
Sprinkle with punctuation.
Serve piping hot.

WRITING: FICTION AND NON-FICTION

Poetry

'Poetry is the best words in the best order.'
Samuel Taylor Coleridge

> When we talk about poetry, we use words like **rhyme**, **assonance**, **rhythm** and **alliteration**. Read on to find out what each word means!

A Good Poem
by Tom Zart

A good poem paints a picture
for both your heart and brain.
It doesn't need a second chance
to make its meaning plain.

RHYME

Words rhyme if their **endings sound the same**, e.g. **cat** and **sat**.

Rhyme is used a lot by poets. It can be hard to tell if two words rhyme just by looking at them. You need to hear the words aloud to know whether or not they rhyme. For example, take the words **night** and **kite**: their endings look different on the page, but they have the same sound when you say them aloud, so they rhyme.

Rhyme at the end of a line

All My Great Excuses
by Kenn Nesbitt

I started on my homework
but my pen ran out of **ink**.
My hamster ate my homework.
My computer's on the **blink**.

I accidentally dropped it
in the soup my mom was **cooking**.
My brother flushed it down the toilet
when I wasn't **looking**.

My mother ran my homework
through the washer and the **dryer**.
An airplane crashed into our house.
My homework caught on **fire**.

Tornadoes blew my notes away.
Volcanoes struck our **town**.
My notes were taken hostage
by an evil killer **clown**.

Some aliens abducted me.
I had a shark **attack**.
A pirate swiped my homework
and refused to give it **back**.

I worked on these excuses
so darned long my teacher **said**,
'I think you'll find it's easier
to do the work **instead**.'

Here is an example of a poem with rhyme at the end of the line.

Rhyme in the middle of a line

Here is an example of rhyme in the middle of a line.

> **Extracts from *The Raven*
> by Edgar Allan Poe**
>
> Once upon a midnight **dreary**, while I pondered, weak and **weary**,
>
> …
>
> While I nodded, nearly **napping**, suddenly there came a **tapping**,

Half-rhyme
Half-rhyme is when words almost or nearly rhyme.
- *bun/ran*

ASSONANCE

Assonance is when **vowel sounds** are repeated.

In the following sentence all the underlined words have the **ee** sound in them, but they are not all spelled with **ee**:
- *Last w<u>ee</u>k, <u>Lee</u> had a p<u>ie</u>ce of ch<u>ee</u>se every night before h<u>e</u> went to sl<u>ee</u>p – to make him dr<u>ea</u>m.*

Who Has Seen the Wind?
by Christina Rosetti

Who has seen the wind?
Neither I nor you:
But when the leaves hang trembling
The wind is passing through.

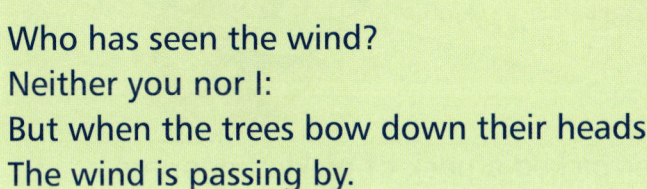

Who has seen the wind?
Neither you nor I:
But when the trees bow down their heads
The wind is passing by.

Can you find examples of assonance in this poem?

RHYTHM

The rhythm of a poem is the **beat** of the words. A lot of poetry follows a pattern of rhythm, where there is a **fixed pattern of syllables** in each line. If a word has too many syllables, it won't fit with the rest of the line.

Hey, diddle, diddle!
The cat and the fiddle,
The cow jumped over the moon.
The little dog laughed
To see such fun
And the dish ran away with the spoon,
the knife, the fork and the cup!

Do you see what happens when one word has too many syllables? There is no longer a fixed pattern – so the line with the long word doesn't fit!

POETRY

ALLITERATION

Alliteration is when **words beginning with the same sound** are used close together. Certain poetry uses a lot of alliteration. Tongue twisters are an example of this.

Here is an example of alliteration.

Peter Piper picked a peck of pickled peppers.
A peck of pickled peppers Peter Piper picked.
If Peter Piper picked a peck of pickled peppers,
How many pickled peppers did Peter Piper pick?

Alliteration is also used in advertising slogans. This is done so that you will remember the name of the product.
- *You'll never put a better bit of butter on your knife! (Country Life butter)*
- *Don't dream it. Drive it. (Jaguar)*

Poets use many tools to create great poems: alliteration, assonance, rhyme, metaphor, onomatopoeia, personification, rhythm and similes. Every time you read a poem, think about how the poem makes you feel and what pictures it creates. You can read a poem over and over again and each time notice something new and interesting in the poem.

WRITING POETRY

Before we try to write some poetry ourselves, let's look at what poets do when they are writing poetry.

Some poets give us a clear and strong picture in our mind when we read their poems. Other poets make their poems give us feelings about something.

Choice of words

Poets take great care when writing their poems and they choose each word carefully. Poets pick the best words and put them in the best place so that the words can describe exactly what things look like, sound or feel like.

Poets **create pictures**, **express moods** and **suggest ideas**. In doing this, they use many different tools.

Similes or **metaphors** are used to compare one thing with something else.
- *Lightning, an angry scar across the dark sky…*

Here, the poet's clever use of a metaphor not only describes what the scene looked like but it also helps to create a frightening mood.

Personification is used to describe an object or idea as if it were a human being.

'Shadow March' by Robert Louis Stevenson is a poem that opens with an example of personification. In this poem, the shadow is described as if it were human.

All round the house is the jet-black night;
It stares through the window-pane;

Sound patterns

Not only do poets chose their words carefully for their meaning, they also choose words for the **sound patterns** they can make. That is why we must always read poems aloud in our head. We can listen for sound patterns, such as **alliteration**, **assonance**, **rhyme**, **onomatopoeia** and **rhythm**.

In the poem 'From a Railway Carriage' by Robert Louis Stevenson, the strong, fast rhythm sounds like the noise of the train moving quickly along the tracks. The poet is using **rhythm** and **rhyme** to make the readers think of a moving train.

From a Railway Carriage
by Robert Louis Stevenson

Faster than fairies, faster than witches,
Bridges and houses, hedges and ditches:
And charging along like troops in a battle,
All through the meadows the horses and cattle;
All of the sights of the hill and the plain
Fly as thick as driving rain;
And ever again, in the wink of an eye,
Painted stations whistle by.

Poem structure and form

Before writing a poem, the poet has to decide the **form** they are going to use. The form of a poem is its shape and structure. There are many different forms of poetry: **haiku**, **limerick**, **free verse**, etc.

Let's look at some different types or forms of poetry.

FORMS OF POETRY

There are many different forms (types) of poetry: **ode**, **concrete poem**, **acrostic poem**, **limerick**, **ballad**, **sonnet**, **haiku**, **free verse**, **cinquain**, **nonsense poem**, **kenning**, etc.

- A **sonnet** is a poem of fourteen lines, which follows a rhyme pattern. Shakespeare wrote some very famous sonnets, e.g. 'Shall I compare thee to a summer's day?'
- A **ballad** can be a poem or a song. It is written to tell a story – often an adventure or a love story. Ballads are usually very long with lots of verses.
- An **ode** is a poem where the writer shares feelings about a person, place or thing that they really like or love.
- A **limerick** is a funny rhyming poem that could start like this: *There was a young man from…* A limerick has five lines and a special rhythm and rhyme pattern.
- A **haiku** is a traditional form of Japanese poetry. Haiku poems have three lines.

PROCESS APPROACH TO WRITING POETRY

1. Making decisions
Before you write you must decide the following:
- Topic: what do you want to write about?
- Audience: who is the writing for?
- Purpose: why are you writing the poem?
- Form: what forms (types) of poetry appeal to you?

It is always easier to write about something you know or about something you have experienced.

2. Planning
Planning means gathering together and ordering your ideas. You should:
- Brainstorm your ideas.
- Describe your ideas with strong and interesting words.
- Organise and group your best ideas.
- Decide what form of poem will best match your ideas: acrostic, concrete, cinquain, etc.

3. Drafting
Poets often write drafts and redrafts of their poems. They add, delete and reorder words before they are happy with the finished poem.

When writing your various drafts:

- Write your revisions in the margins.
- Write on every second line so you will have space to add extra words or sentences later.
- Hunt for the right word, neatly crossing out a word and replacing it with a better or stronger word.
- Always cross out an idea or a word instead of rubbing it out: you may change your mind and want to use the first idea again later on.

Check your draft by asking yourself these questions:
- Do I want to cross out or add a word?
- Do I want to make changes that would improve my poem?
- Have I read my draft to another person or group?

If you have read your draft to another person or group, take note of the ideas and suggestions they give you. You could ask them the following questions:
- Did you enjoy the poem? Why?
- What did you think of the rhythm?
- What did you think of the rhyme (if it rhymes – remember, not all poems have to rhyme)?
- What did you think of the choice of words?
- How did the poem make you feel?

4. Responding, revising and proofreading

At this stage, your poem is nearly complete. You have discussed your poem with others and you are now satisfied that your ideas are written in the form you wanted.

It is now time to proofread your poem to make sure that everything is correct and clear: spelling, punctuation, grammar and layout. After proofreading, your poem should have no mistakes and it should be easily read by others.

5. Presenting and publishing

After working hard on drafting and redrafting, it is now time to publish your poem. Before you share your poem with an audience, you need to ask yourself the following questions:
- Will I use the computer or my own handwriting?
- Will I share my poem in book form, on the school notice board or in the school magazine? Or will I read it aloud?

6. Reflecting

Before starting a new poem, it is a good idea to look over the poem you have just completed. Ask yourself the following questions:
- What was my poem about?
- How did I start?
- Where did I get my ideas?
- Did I change my ideas while writing?
- What did I find hard? What did I find easy? Why?
- How do I feel about the finished poem?
- Did I enjoy writing the poem?

It is also a good idea to talk to your teacher about your poems. Think about the things that you did really well and the things that you need to work on.

USING POETRY TO WRITE POETRY

This is a great way to learn how to write your own poetry:

1. Choose a poem that you really like.
2. Blank out parts of the poem. This might be every second line, a word in every line, a whole verse – you decide!
3. Now play around with the blank spaces, inserting different words. In this way, you will create a new poem.
4. When you have completed your version of the poem, choose a new title for it.

> Let's try this with 'The Sound Collector' by Roger McGough. Leave the first and last verses as they are and insert lots of blank spaces in the middle of the poem.

In the middle of Roger McGough's poem, he lists all the different **sounds** that the sound collector has taken from his house, e.g. 'The **hissing** of the **frying pan**'. Now that these objects and their sounds have been taken out, you can insert your own. Use your imagination!

The Sound Collector
by Roger McGough

A stranger called this morning
Dressed all in black and grey
Put every sound into a bag
And carried them away.

The _____ of the _____ (a)
The _____ of the _____ (b) rhyme
The _____ of the _____ (c)
The _____ of the _____ (b) rhyme

The _____ of the _____ (d)
The _____ of the _____ (e) rhyme
The _____ of the _____ (f)
The _____ of the _____ (e) rhyme

A stranger called this morning
He didn't leave his name
Left us only silence
Life will never be the same.

> Here is an example of using poems to write poems! It is 'The Sound Collector' by Roger McGough – and this version has been written by Emma Cowley.

Using Poems to Write Poems

Emma Cowley
Fourth Class

Scoil Eoin Naofa
NS
Co. Cork

'My version of "The Sound Collector" by Roger McGough' now entitled 'The School Sound Collector'.

A stranger called this morning
Dressed in black and grey
Put every sound into a bag
And carried them away.

The ringing of the bell
The noise of the children talking
The bounce of the ball
The steps of the children walking

The squeaking of the markers
The sweet voices of the children singing
The happy sound of laughter
The sound of the doorbell ringing

A stranger called this morning
He didn't leave his name
Left us only silence
Life will never be the same.

ACROSTIC POEM

An **acrostic** poem is one where the first letters of each line come together to form a word, phrase or sentence. This word, phrase or sentence is usually the title of the poem.

You can write an acrostic poem based on your name, a favourite hobby or anything that is important to you!

Titanic

Tragic night
Icebergs plenty
Tonnes of metal sink
Alone in deep icy water
Now sits quietly
In dark tomb
Cold and rusting

Father

Football
Acrobat
Thoughtful
Huggable
Energetic
Reliable

> Here is an example of an acrostic poem entitled 'Emotions'. It was written by Ciarán Cotter.

Acrostic

Ciarán Cotter
Fifth Class

Scoil Eoin NS
Ballincollig
Co. Cork

'Emotions'

Everyone feels them
Makes you feel happy
Or sad, angry or worried
Tricked, frightened or frustrated
Irate, disappointed or excited
Overjoyed, embarrassed or ashamed
Never ending
Stays for eternity

Top tips for writing an acrostic poem

1. Choose an interesting **topic**.
2. **Brainstorm** and write down all of your ideas.
3. Choose a **title** for the poem.
4. **Single words** are easiest to work with.
5. **Spell out** the title, writing **each letter in a separate box** and arranging the boxes in a **vertical** line.
6. Examine the letters one by one.

7. For each letter, write down any words or phrases that **begin with that letter**.
8. The words and phrases must be **linked to your topic**.
9. Pick out the **best word** or phrase for each line of poetry.
10. The acrostic writing frame will help you with this process.

ACROSTIC POEM WRITING FRAME

1. Decide
2. Plan it!
3. Draft it!
4. Check and change it!
5. Publish it!
6. Think about it!

Your name: _____
Date of writing: _____

Topic Choose a topic.

Title Choose a title.

Write your poem

- Write the title down in a vertical line, putting each letter in a box.
- Use each letter as the first letter for each line of the poem.

CONCRETE POEM

A concrete poem takes on the **shape** of its subject. A concrete poem is also called a shape poem. Shape poems are very striking. When you see a concrete poem on the page, it is actually shaped like the topic of the poem!

Here is an example of a concrete poem entitled 'Tigers'. It was written by Dean Kearney.

Concrete Poem

Dean Kearney	Scoil Eoin NS	'Tigers'
Fourth Class	Ballincollig	
	Co. Cork	

They come in all shapes and sizes,
colours orange and white.
If you saw one face to face you'd
surely get a fright.
Although they're surely
memorable on the jungle floor.
With their piercing eyes and open
jaws you will hear a mighty ROAR.

Top tips for writing a concrete poem

1. Choose an interesting **topic**.
2. **Brainstorm** and write down all of your ideas.
3. Choose a **title** for the poem.
4. Think about the **shape** that your poem will take, e.g. a poem entitled 'Ball' would need to take the shape of a ball on the page.
5. Now that you have decided on a shape, you must **arrange the words** so that they take this shape on the page.
6. **Draw** the shape or outline on your page before you fill in any words.
7. Choose the words or phrases that will **fit properly** into the shape.
8. Remember that the words and phrases must fit into the shape – but they must also be **linked to the topic**!
9. This is a bit like a jigsaw puzzle: all the pieces must all fit together properly. You might need to **write many drafts** before you have a final concrete poem.
10. The concrete poem writing frame will help you with this process.

CONCRETE POEM WRITING FRAME

1. Decide
2. Plan it!
3. Draft it!
4. Check and change it!
5. Publish it!
6. Think about it!

Your name: _____
Date of writing: _____

Topic Choose a topic.

Title Choose a title.

Write your poem

Shape Draw the shape or outline of the poem on the page before you fill in any words or phrases.

CINQUAIN

The modern cinquain is a five-line poem. The structure is as follows:

- **Line 1** 1 **noun**: the title or name of the topic
- **Line 2** 2 **adjectives**: describing words connected to the topic
- **Line 3** 3 **verbs**: doing words, describing the topic's actions
- **Line 4** 4 **words describing** a feeling or thought about the topic
- **Line 5** 1 **noun**: a synonym for the title, another name for the subject

Here is an example of a cinquain entitled 'Funfair'. It was written by Nathan Brydon.

Tiger
Sleek, graceful
Hiding, hunting, running
Happy to be free
Cat

Cinquain

Nathan Brydon Fourth Class	Scoil Eoin NS Ballincollig Co. Cork	'Funfair'

Funfair
Loud, fun
Running, jumping, sliding
Entertaining for small kids
Carnival

Top tips for writing a cinquain

1. Choose an interesting **topic** or subject for the cinquain.
2. **Brainstorm** and write down all of your ideas about the topic.
3. Choose **one noun** as the title for your cinquain.
4. Ask yourself questions about the topic and how it affects the **senses**. What does it look, sound, feel, taste and smell like?
5. List all the **adjectives** that could be used to describe your topic.
6. Think about what your topic can do. What **actions** can it perform? List all the **verbs** that could be used to describe the action of your topic.
7. Write down how your topic affects your **feelings**. What emotions do you have about the topic?
8. Use a thesaurus to list all of the **synonyms** for your topic.
9. Select which words you want to include in your cinquain.
10. The cinquain writing frame will help you with this process.

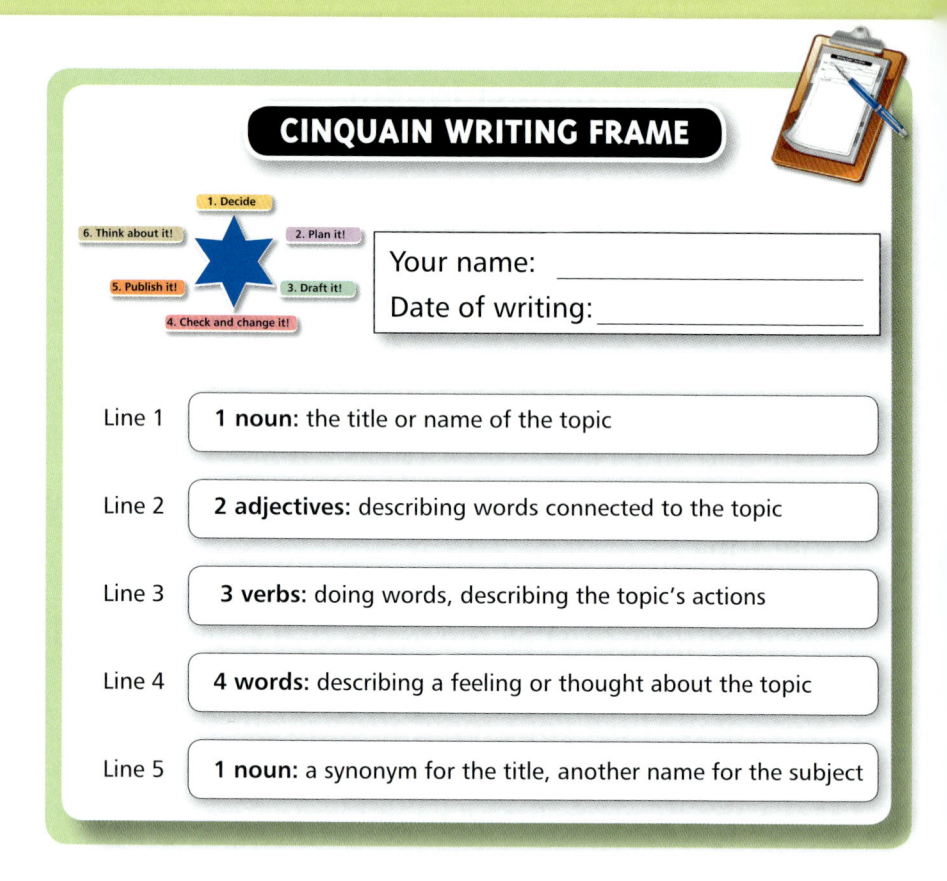

CINQUAIN WRITING FRAME

1. Decide
2. Plan it!
3. Draft it!
4. Check and change it!
5. Publish it!
6. Think about it!

Your name: _____
Date of writing: _____

Line 1 — **1 noun:** the title or name of the topic

Line 2 — **2 adjectives:** describing words connected to the topic

Line 3 — **3 verbs:** doing words, describing the topic's actions

Line 4 — **4 words:** describing a feeling or thought about the topic

Line 5 — **1 noun:** a synonym for the title, another name for the subject

FREE VERSE

Free verse poetry is 'free' from the normal rules of poetry. Free verse poems don't rhyme and have no definite beat or rhythm. So when you are writing free verse, feel *free* to have fun and create. There are no rules!

When writing **free verse,** you can put words together in all sorts of ways. You can be **very imaginative**. You can also choose any topic. Just have fun putting words together so that your reader gets a clear picture of what you are talking about.

If you want to write free verse, it helps to first write a few paragraphs about your topic. You can then use these paragraphs to create a piece of free verse.

If you were to write about autumn, you could say:

Autumn is a season that brings Halloween to people, and sleep to some animals.

If you wanted to turn this text into free verse, it could look something like this:

Autumn

Autumn, autumn, autumn!
A season that brings
Halloween to people
And sleep to some animals.

Autumn, autumn, autumn!

Here is an example of a free verse piece entitled 'All-Ireland Final'. It was written by Ríain Brennan.

Free Verse

Ríain Brennan	Scoil Eoin NS	'All-Ireland Final'
Fifth Class	Ballincollig	
	Co. Cork	

All the nerves
Lots of pressure
Loads of tension
Ireland watch
Really interested
Excited
Liam McCarthy's heading to a county
And absolutely no team, no player –
No one – wants to lose. They want to win!
Dramatic game; come on the Cats!
Finally it's over
It ends as a win to Kilkenny
Next, the lifting of the trophy
All the fans cheering:
Liam McCarthy's coming home!

Top tips for writing free verse

1. Choose an interesting **topic** or subject.
2. Your free verse could tell a story or describe a person, animal, feeling or object.
3. **Brainstorm** and write down all of your ideas about the topic.
4. Use your ideas to write a **paragraph** about your topic.
5. Ask yourself questions about the topic and how it affects the **senses**. What does it look, sound, feel, taste and smell like?
6. List all the **adjectives** that could be used to describe your topic.
7. When you have written the draft paragraph, **break it into lines** or **stanzas**.
8. Revise the lines until they look and sound right to you. Write as many **drafts** of the lines as you want.
9. Remove any unnecessary words and use a thesaurus to choose more powerful **synonyms**.
10. The free verse writing frame will help you with this process.

FREE VERSE WRITING FRAME

1. Decide
2. Plan it!
3. Draft it!
4. Check and change it!
5. Publish it!
6. Think about it!

Your name: _____
Date of writing: _____

Topic — Choose a topic.

Title — _____

Paragraph — Write a paragraph (or more) about your topic.

Lines of poetry — Choose the words or phrases to include in your free verse.
Arrange them into lines and stanzas.

Topic Suggestions

Recount
- Our school trip
- My summer holidays
- How I spent last Christmas
- The best party ever!
- My first pet
- The worst day I ever had
- Our day at the zoo
- Last year's All-Ireland Final
- My birthday
- Granny's visit to our house

Procedure
- How to make a pizza
- Step-by-step magic trick
- How to wrap a birthday present
- Recipe for a fruit smoothie
- How to play hopscotch
- Step-by-step guide to feeding your dog
- How to use finger multiplication to remember your times tables
- Step-by-step guide to planting seeds
- How to make a St Brigid's cross
- Directions to Granddad's house

Information reports
- Emperor penguins
- Katie Taylor
- Italy
- Swallows
- Mount Everest
- Co. Kerry
- Bears in the wild
- The life cycle of a frog

Explanation
- How do plants make their food?
- Why do animals hibernate?
- How does an aeroplane fly?
- How are pencils made?
- How do chicken eggs hatch?
- Why do we put up Christmas trees?
- How are guide dogs trained?
- Why do cats have whiskers?
- How are crisps made?
- How is Easter celebrated in Europe?

Persuasion
- Healthy eating is important
- Schoolbags should not be so heavy
- Nobody should be homeless
- Mobile phones are good
- Bullying is very dangerous
- Too much junk food is bad
- Aliens exist
- Global warming must stop
- Ghosts don't exist
- Endangered animals must be saved

Discussion
- Is TV bad for us?
- Are zoos good or bad for animals?
- Should children choose their own bedtimes?
- Is it good to have advertisements for toys on the TV at Christmas?
- Should mobile phones be banned in schools?
- Is Ireland a nice place to live?
- Should children play video games?
- Should animals be made to perform in circuses?
- Are school holidays too long?
- Is Friday the best day of the week?

Response
- My meal in a local restaurant
- The play I went to see
- Last year's St Patrick's Day parade
- A new TV programme
- The latest album by my favourite band
- An Oscar-winning film
- The concert I attended last week
- A book I have just read
- The hotel we stayed in last summer
- A new comic book series

Narrative
Narrative writing can be about absolutely anything! Here are just some ideas to get you started.
- Horror story: V is for Vampire
- Adventure story: Hidden Treasure
- Fantasy story: War on Pluto
- Mystery: The Suspicious Stone
- Historical: Escaping the Famine
- Science fiction: Robodog and Cybercat
- Humorous: Drooler the Dog Drives the Bus
- Myth or legend: Queen Hannah and the Enchanted Wood
- Fairy story: The Goblin of Greystones

Poetry
Poetry can be about absolutely anything. Let your imagination run free!
Here are some ideas to get you started.
- Acrostic poem: Mother
- Concrete poem: Home
- Cinquain: Circus
- Free verse: Snow

INDEX

A
acronyms, 56–7
acrostic poem, 198–200
adjectives, 16–19
adverbs, 20–1
alliteration, 188
antonyms, 26
apostrophes, 63–5
articles, 22
assonance, 186–7
autobiography, 47

B
ballad, 191
biography, 47
blurb, 48–9
brackets, 59

C
capital letters, 53–4
chapters, 49
characters, 178–80
cinquain, 204–6
colons, 66
commas, 68–70
compound words, 30
concrete poem, 201–3
conjunctions, 24
connectives, 46–7

D
dashes, 59–60
dialogue, 45
direct questions, 58
direct speech, 36–7
discussion, 148–54
drafting, 79–81

E
emails, 102–3
envelopes, addressing, 101
exclamation marks, 60–1
exclamations, 25
explanation, 134–9
extracts, 50

F
formal language, 86–7
formal letters, 87–94
free verse, 206–10
full stops, 55–7

H
haiku, 191
homonyms, 27
homophones, 27
hyphens, 62

I
idioms, 28
imagery, 32
indirect questions, 58
indirect speech, 36–7
informal language, 86–7
informal letters, 95–100
information reports, 128–33
initialisms, 56–7
inverted commas, 71–2

L
language, formal or informal, 86–7
leaflets, 146–8
letters, 87–100
limerick, 191

M
metaphors, 34

N
narrative, 159–81
newspaper report, 116–20
nouns, 5–9
novel, 47–8

O
ode, 191
onomatopoeia, 34–5

P
paragraphs, 42–4
parts of a text, 49–50
parts of speech, 2–4
personification, 33
persuasion, 140–5
poetry, forms of, 191
poetry, writing, 189–91
posters, 146–8
prefixes, 30
prepositions, 22–4
procedure, 121–7
process approach, 78–83
  poetry, 192–5
pronouns, 10–11
proverbs, 29
punctuation, 52–3
  summary, 75–6
punctuation poems, 73–4

Q
question marks, 57–8
questions, types of, 58
quotations, 50

R
recount, 104–15
response, 154–9
  review, 49, 154–9
rhyme, 184–6
rhythm, 187

S
semicolons, 67
sentences, 38–41
similes, 32
sonnet, 191
sound patterns, 190
suffixes, 31
synonyms, 26
synopsis, 48

T
table of contents, 49–50
text, parts of, 49–50
texts, types of, 47–9
topic suggestions, 212–14

V
verbs, 12–15

W
writing, process approach to, 78–83
writing frames, 84–5